Talk to Yourself

TALK TO YOURSELF
Experiencing Intrapersonal Communication

Genelle Austin-Lett
Illinois Central College

Jan Sprague
Waubonsee Community College

HOUGHTON MIFFLIN COMPANY
Boston · Atlanta · Dallas · Geneva, Ill.
Hopewell, N.J. · Palo Alto · London

Printed in the U.S.A.

Library of Congress Catalog Card Number: 75-31037

ISBN: 0-395-18576-9

with much love to
our parents
and
Scott, Susan, David, Cynthia, and Laurie
—in spite of sibling rivalry

CONTENTS

When the mind is thinking, it is talking to itself.
—Plato

PREFACE

Talk to Yourself is an introduction to intrapersonal communication, communication with yourself. We see this text as a versatile tool. It can be used as an intrapersonal communication textbook with the reader as the only sender and receiver of information, choosing which private and confidential journal entries and personal responses to individual exercises are to be included in the workbook. Or, *Talk to Yourself* may be used to bridge the gap between intrapersonal and interpersonal communication. The group exercises generate personal development as a result of interaction with others; and, conversely, as self-awareness increases, students become more willing to share their thoughts with others. As students learn more about how others view themselves, each individual's self-concept is affected. To record this essential growth, pages are provided at the back of the book for journal entries with probing questions to stimulate responses.

Selected readings which reinforce and extend the content have been chosen for the conclusion of each chapter. In some cases the readings provide a viewpoint that differs from ours in its approach to the concepts of intrapersonal communication. And to further expand the student's knowledge in this area each reading is followed by an annotated bibliography.

We recommend *Talk to Yourself* for use in the basic speech course, but others have suggested that it be used for courses in intrapersonal communication, interpersonal communication, persuasion, business management, human potential, and counseling. It may easily be used wherever there is a need for self-improvement or a desire for self-examination. However, this is not a textbook on lay psychology, positive thinking, or psychoanalysis. It is an introduction to intrapersonal communication, to be used to stimulate thinking about how and why individuals shape and communicate their personal worlds.

ACKNOWLEDGMENTS

We wish to thank Susan Gail Blomquist for her creative suggestions and preliminary work on graphics and Carol Jeanne Meister for her hours spent typing, proofing, and probing. We also wish to thank our students at Illinois Central College and Waubonsee Community College who tested and evaluated the exercises and journal assignments. A special note of thanks to Don Marine who, recognizing the importance of intrapersonal communication, encouraged us to write this textbook.

We have greatly appreciated suggestions and recommendations from our reviewers: John Muchmore, William Rainey Harper College, Palatine, Ill.; James Pence, University of North Carolina, Chapel Hill, N.C.; Barbara Strain, San Antonio College, San Antonio, Tex.; Nil Whittington, Temple Junior College, Temple, Tex. And we warmly thank Isa Engleberg, Prince George's County College, Largo, Md., who has given us much support, input, constructive criticism, and help from our first outline to the final copy.

We would also like to express our appreciation to those individuals whose lives we have shared and whose appearances in examples we deliberately planned. To those other unnamed individuals who were a continuing source of ideas and inspiration—thank you.

Man's mind stretched to a new idea never goes back to its original dimensions.

—Oliver Wendell Holmes

TO THE STUDENT

How long has it been since you last looked in a mirror? Were you brushing your teeth, combing your hair, or admiring your body? How frequently would you stand in front of a mirror if it projected your inner thoughts? Would you tend to avoid those details and be grateful that no one else can see them? If your answer is yes, you are like many other people who can look at the surface of what they are, but who find it difficult to look at what really makes them unique individuals.

The purpose of this text is to help you remove your mask or facade in order to observe the "real" you. As you understand who you are and where you are going, you will be able to communicate better with others. Why? Because any attempt to improve communication must begin with improving intrapersonal communication; the self is the center of all communication. G. H. Mead, a renowned psychologist, views the development of self-identity or self-concept as the product of social interaction. Mead emphasizes the importance of face-to-face interpersonal communication—how you respond to others and how they in turn respond to you. Through your experiences with others, you learn about yourself. Each interchange gives you cues about how others see you.* So we are not overstepping the bounds of intrapersonal communication when we ask you to share what you are learning about yourself with others. It is interaction that helps you perceive correctly or incorrectly who you are.

To get the most out of this text you have to put YOU into it. If goals and objectives are to be of value in any course or experience, you must set them yourself, work to accomplish them, and ultimately judge the progress that you make. This process of goal-setting and self-examination involves self-discipline. Some people can easily identify what they think about themselves. For others it is a process of prying, a gradual opening to see what masks or roles conceal. Nevertheless, you need to motivate yourself while you work toward improved intrapersonal communication. You are in the best position to judge personal communication assets and liabilities. Through your experiences you have developed feelings of satisfaction or dissatisfaction in daily communication encounters.

The text is organized to help you set and achieve your goals. The objectives at the beginning of each chapter are guideposts to help you understand and utilize the material that follows. Integrate the pictures and quotations found throughout the text with your thinking about your self-concept.

In each chapter you will be referred to journal exercises. You can record the entries in the area provided for the journal at the back of the book, or you can create your own journal. The journal is your personal, introspective analysis, and you should consider the journal entries as a catalyst. They should stimulate you to record other feelings and ideas, so that you can adapt this book to your needs. Think critically and creatively about your goals, desires, and needs. Pursue your own course of self-study based on the ideas we recommend for journal entries. Supplement these assigned journal entries with informal entries detailing your intrapersonal communication experiences in and out of the classroom.

Other exercises are designed for individual or group participation. All responses to the individual exercises are to be recorded directly in the text, and your instructor may ask you to share this information. Occasionally, the content of exercises and journal entries will overlap, but your journal comments are your private record of your intrapersonal communication growth and need not be shared with anyone.

The group exercises are for classroom or small group interaction. There is no write-in space provided for entries dealing with interpersonal communication activities, but your reactions may be recorded as additional journal comments. It is important to answer all the questions within the text, maintain an inquiring mind, and formulate probes of your own. Get into the habit of talking to yourself about yourself, and of keeping a written record as you reach for self-knowledge and satisfaction in intrapersonal communication.

* G. H. Mead, *Mind, Self, and Society* (Chicago: University of Chicago Press, 1934), pp. 144-146.

We want you to make your text entries and journal a part of your life. Keep in mind that you are the center of the course. The content of your text is what you choose to put into it. The book in essence becomes you, because it is your self-examination and self-disclosure that make this book uniquely yours.

TO THE INSTRUCTOR

Designed as a supplementary textbook for introductory communication courses, *Talk to Yourself* provides theoretical material, numerous individual and group exercises, and additional readings. It can fill a seven-week study or be condensed to suit a three-week course unit without compromising the goals of (1) providing sufficient theoretical explanation for the student to understand the operation of intrapersonal communication, and (2) structuring experiences in which self-examination and self-disclosure can occur.

When you want additional consideration of theory, the annotated bibliography directs students to primary source material. There should be enough exercises and journal entries for you to choose those that supply the intrapersonal communication activities you think your students need and that also complement later course content.

The individual exercise is the student's personal response to the material in the text. This exercise differs from the journal entry in that you may call on the students to share some of their exercise comments with the class or small group, letting them compare similarities and differences. The students will record the individual exercises in the text.

The group exercises purposely require the student to practice self-examination and self-disclosure in interpersonal, small group, and public communication formats. We hope that through these formats, the student will avoid the erroneous conclusion that intrapersonal communication operates in isolation and that the self-concept is immune from influence or modification by others. The formats also make obvious the assertion that intrapersonal communication operates as the basis of communication behavior on all other levels. Further, the emphasis on the public experience of self-disclosure meets our students' expectations that, at the conclusion of a speech communication course, they will have acquired new skills in group communication and public speaking. Many of the group exercises can be accomplished with either small groups or the whole class. We vary our approach depending on total class size, orientation of the course, and interests of the students. Three group exercises include criteria for evaluation.

Success with the individual and group exercises depends on establishing an atmosphere of mutual trust and sharing in the classroom. For us this has meant that no exercise is of value only for students. As teachers, we have participated in group self-disclosure exercises, reacted in our journals, shared our self-concept collages, and subjected our beliefs to challenge.

The journals make the students primarily responsible for their own progress. Teachers often fear that students are not motivated toward self-direction. This can be a time to bridge that gap of trust. As the instructor, you have the option of promoting their motivation by announcing that journals will be collected several times during the course. Their content is strictly confidential and grading is out of the question, as it could easily inhibit the student's self-examination. But you should use this opportunity to suggest possible goals for the student and to compliment or reward those students undertaking comprehensive self-evaluation.

One more invaluable tool for self-examination is videotape. You can play back tapes of the classroom experiences to recall their verbal content and to analyze closely the accompanying nonverbal behavior, which allows the student more information on which to make evaluations.

The following course suggestion is a rough idea of what can be done and a variation of what we have used. A three-week program using *Talk To Yourself* would include a complete reading of the text and some well-planned uses of exercises. The following is an example of a three-week program:

Week One: Read chapters one and two. Use the wallet identification exercise, at least one group self-disclosure exercise, and the exercise on improving perceptual skills.
Week Two: Read chapter three. Include the speech on challenge to belief.
Week Three: Read chapters four and five. Use the exercise about symbols, attitudes, and judgments, and the exercise on labeling and secret sharing.

For a five- to seven-week program, read the entire book and include some additional readings. You might use the speech on challenge to belief with the entire class and not just small groups. Or you could incorporate and enjoy all the exercises and watch your students' as well as your own growth.

Either of these approaches to the text is workable with a speech class in which you include intrapersonal communication. We understand that some exercises work better for one instructor than another. We have our pet exercises, and others who have used the materials have found other favorites. Our recommendation is that you try the exercises with which you are comfortable and modify the others with any additions that you might discover.

To venture causes anxiety, but not to venture is to lose one's self . . . . And to venture in the highest sense is precisely to become conscious of one's self.
—Sören Kierkegaard

1. SELF-CONCEPT APPROACH TO INTRAPERSONAL COMMUNICATION

OBJECTIVES   In this chapter we ask you to do the following:

1. Examine who you think you are.

2. Identify your imagined self.

3. Consider how the attitudes of others toward you influence your self-concept.

4. Recognize how your physical and mental competencies influence your self-concept.

5. List personal assets and liabilities that affect your ability to communicate.

6. Discover the interaction of your attitudes, values, and beliefs in your intrapersonal communication.

For centuries human beings have struggled to answer the questions "Who am I?" and "Where am I going?" Our literature, music, and art reflect this search for true identity. Individuality has become a cherished fact of our existence. Then how important it is that we recognize self-concept as the basis of communication.

Intrapersonal communication should not be confused with interpersonal communication, which deals with two or more persons interacting with each other. Intrapersonal communication focuses on the importance of individual behavior—it is concerned with what we think about ourselves. Such thoughts are unique, for there is no way anyone else can experience this thinking or reflecting process. It is exclusively personal because we can never separate our opinions and beliefs from our perceptions of communication events. Self-concept is the directing force for this inner process.

The Kierkegaard quotation at the beginning of this chapter mentions that to seek out one's self causes anxiety. This is often true. As we strive to get a better understanding of who we are, we try to be honest with ourselves. Knowing that we are able to see our strong and weak points can produce anxiety. Yet Plato asserts, "The unexamined life isn't worth living." What do we have to lose in finding out who we really are? As a first step, try Journal Exercise 1 at the back of the book.

Self-concept includes all of our perceptions of our physical, social, and psychological competencies that have evolved through our experiences with ourselves, our interactions with others, and our position in a specific cultural and social environment. Self-discovery and self-examination are tools we use to find our self-concept. Through self-disclosure we discuss with others our internalized thinking about ourselves.

David Johnson, in his book *Reaching Out*, defines self-disclosure as "revealing how you are reacting to the present situation and giving any information about the past that is relevant to understanding how you are reacting to the present."[1] Keep in mind that self-disclosure is a process and that it is ongoing; it is not something that you do today and then forget about tomorrow. It should become a way of communicating. Self-disclosure occurs when you openly and honestly communicate yourself to others. This honest exchange allows for the sharing of personal thoughts. But you should not totally bare your most precious thoughts. If you get too personal, you may feel uncomfortable and make others feel equally uncomfortable. This sharing should not be a painful unveiling. You should share as much as you are willing to and as much as you can cope with adequately. View it as an opportunity to communicate what you are finding out about yourself.

This type of disclosure allows more open and spontaneous communication to develop. As a result, you gain a better understanding of each other and of how belief and value systems differ and operate in personal growth. Such

---

[1] David W. Johnson, *Reaching Out: Interpersonal Effectiveness and Self-Actualization* (Englewood Cliffs, N.J.: Prentice-Hall, 1972), p. 10.

understanding tends to give increased satisfaction with life and opens the doors for better interpersonal relationships.[2]

However, some people neglect intrapersonal communication, citing the risks involved. They typically react by saying, "It is nobody's business who I am or what I think." But such a statement does tell you something about their self-concept. Maybe it is not anyone's business to know what they are thinking. Why should you pry into an individual's innermost thoughts? Aren't these thoughts sacred? What we're asking is that you know *why* you do not want to share your thoughts, *why* you do not want others to communicate theirs to you. The answer will reveal even more about your self-concept. Perhaps you feel that if you tell someone something personal, the whole world will hear about it. Another risk is negative feedback; that is, people may not respond at all to what you have said. Some take this lack of response as rejection and give up the whole process of disclosure. Or you may feel that if you expose one weakness, others will think you are still hiding more.

You establish a relationship by disclosing your reactions to events or to what other people say or do. Without self-disclosure it is difficult to form close personal relationships. Your strength lies in your willingness to take risks in your relationships, with the intention of building better relationships and improving your self-concept.[3]

We could continue building cases for and against self-disclosure, but the fact remains that you still have to live with yourself and deal with others. There is always room for change and innovation in your mental life-style. Basically all people have a desire to grow and be successful. Look at self-disclosure as bringing you one step closer to this goal.

Exercise 1
Self-Disclosure

In this individual or group exercise, decide what questions will help others obtain an accurate perception of you. Write down those questions and turn them in to your instructor. Draw one of these disclosure questions from a box that will be passed around the room. Read the question aloud and answer it as fully as is comfortable for you. At the end of the session, the instructor will collect the questions to use with the next group of students.

Some questions we've used include:

1. What gives you a sense of security? Do you feel secure in this class? Why or why not?

2. What is necessary to establish trust? Do you trust others? Whom do you trust in this class?

3. What makes you feel uncomfortable? Why? What do you do about it?

4. What makes you angry? When was the last time you were angry? Why? What did you do about it?

5. What makes you happy? Why? What situation(s) bring about this feeling?

[2] John R. Wenburg and William W. Wilmot, *The Personal Communication Process* (New York: John Wiley & Sons, 1973), pp. 218–220.
[3] Ibid.

6. Are you afraid of people? Why or why not?

7. What is involved in loving someone? Do you feel loved? If so, why?

8. What is your outlook for your future? (Anticipation? Fear?) Why? Can you change?

9. What does friendship mean to you? Do you have many friends? Are you a good friend to others?

10. Are you satisfied with who you think you are? Why or why not?

11. What does the word *commitment* mean to you? How does it affect your life?

12. What two things would you like to change about yourself? Why?

13. If you had two weeks left to live, what would you do with your life, and why?

14. Is it difficult for you to say "I'm sorry"? When was the last time you told someone that you were sorry? Why were you sorry?

15. Who or what is a driving force in your experience?

16. What does success mean to you? Why? Are you successful?

17. If you had two wishes, what would you want? Why? What do they reveal about your self-concept?

18. Do you get depressed easily? If so, why? If not, how do you avoid depression?

19. Why are you going to school? Who has influenced you to go to school?

20. Are you lonely? Why or why not? How do you cope with loneliness?

Up to this point we have been concerned with defining intrapersonal communication, self-concept, and self-disclosure. Now consider the four ways you learn about yourself: (1) how you view yourself in the roles you play, (2) how you fantasize what you will become, (3) how you think others see you, and (4) how your physical and mental competences shape your attitudes, values, and beliefs.

THE SELF I THINK I AM
Examine your thinking about yourself in much the same way that you would look in a mirror to check that a mask is ready for the outside world.

> *Life is like an onion; you peel off one*
> *layer at a time, and sometimes you weep.*
>
> —*Carl Sandburg*

The comparison of your thoughts to a reflection in a mirror is an important metaphor for understanding the characteristics that constitute a self-concept. Reflection is an effortless process. There's nothing difficult about standing in front of a mirror and seeing your image—it's just there. The

Jean-Claude LeJeune, Stock Boston

mental reflecting process may appear more difficult to examine if you refuse or neglect to look at yourself in your mental mirror and examine what's there. As you look in your mirror, how do you view yourself? What roles have you assumed in life? Don't make judgments about the image yet.

Exercise 2

Roles and Personality Characteristics

In this individual exercise, list in the left-hand column the roles you have assumed in life—student, daughter, father, football player, wife, teacher, cook, and so on. In the right-hand column start listing your personality characteristics (what you perceive yourself to be)—honest, intelligent, handsome, humorous, lonely, timid, depressed, and so on.

Roles

Personality characteristics

Which roles typify who you think you are? Are there some roles that require more responsibility than others? Match your personality characteristics with your roles. For example, one role might be that of student; the personality characteristic you match with it could be conscientious or haphazard, bored or enthusiastic. You may find that the same personality characteristics are common in many roles. As a nurse, perhaps you rate yourself dependable. You may extend this same trait of reliability to your role as a parent. This suggests that you act consistently in many aspects of your life.

What do differences in personality characteristics between roles suggest? For example, consider a doctor whose patient and compassionate bedside manner gives patients confidence in his ability to heal, but who is unconcerned with his own family's problems and short-tempered when he is asked to help around the house. What might be the cause of this shift in personality across roles?

You should start to get a better understanding of who you are as you examine how you perceive yourself. Don't be afraid to look at the qualities that you don't want anyone to know about. Find out why you want to conceal them. This inquiry will give you deeper insight into your self-concept.

It is true that both likes and dislikes operate in your belief systems, but it is also true that they can be stumbling blocks to finding out who you really are. In your mental mirror start examining the good and bad traits that your reflection comprises. Somewhere inside you exists the real self. However, you may be hiding behind masks or playing roles so that you camouflage your true identity. But why? Are you afraid to tell people who you are? Have you managed to build such tight walls around your inner self that you don't even know who you are? It is what you are becoming through self-discovery—not what you are right now—that is important in your personal growth. We like to think of the emerging self-concept as a process of change.

Psychologist Carl Rogers emphasizes the importance of viewing yourself in the process of "becoming" a person—an individual ever changing as new experiences expand your world. John Powell reiterates this belief with his definition of self-concept: if you are anything as a person it's what you "think, judge, feel, value, honor, esteem, love, hate, fear, desire, hope for, believe, and [are] committed to."[4] These qualities are not static but are ever changing as you process information about yourself, others, and your environment. This self-examination can be one of the biggest steps in your life. If you can face what you truly are and what you have contributed to your self-concept, you will be able to grow and, possibly, change.

Rogers further explains, "When I accept myself as I am, I change, and when I accept others as they are, they change." Presently, you will be concerned with the first part of this statement. Rogers is not suggesting that you list the changes you feel are necessary. But he is stressing that when you accept what you find out about yourself, you will naturally change. You become more at peace and at ease; you accept the fact that you are becoming, and your understanding of the important role of self-concept increases.

Getting a better understanding of your self-concept calls for an open mind. Have you ever tried to take something with your hands already full? Clearly something has to go, and you have to decide what it will be. But this decision is not difficult if you want the new thing badly enough. Grasping a new idea or concept of yourself is very similar. Thoughts loaded with human limitations and reservations, doubts, grudges, and depression have to be cleared away to make room for the new concept.

Now is a good time to remove your mask. Stand in front of your mirror and let the real you shine out. This story illustrates the type of discovery that you may make. A woman had been given what she thought to be a homely art object by a good friend as a housewarming gift. For months she kept this object on a shelf in full view so that her friend could see it. One day when she moved it slightly, a slip of paper fell out that read, "Hang in the sunlight for the best results." She did this, and the object became a beautiful and brilliant contribution to her living room. Bringing it out of its corner into the sunlight gave it a dimension and a beauty that it hadn't had before. So it is with viewing yourself in a new light. As you understand who you are, you add dimension to your self-concept.

> *Accept me as I am—only then will we discover*
> *each other.*   —*Frederico Fellini*

[4] John Powell, *Why Am I Afraid to Tell You Who I Am?* (Chicago: Argus Communications, 1969), p. 8.

Exercise 3

Communication Assets and Liabilities

As an individual exercise to help uncover the experiences that have caused you to make judgments about yourself, prepare a list of your communication assets in the left-hand column. In the right-hand column list your communication liabilities.

                    Assets   *Liabilities*

Using the questions that follow as probes, describe your experiences and include your reasons for your answers.

1. What do you see when you look in the mirror?

2. What do you hear when you open your mouth?

3. Do you ever start talking before you decide what you want to say?

4. Do other people seem to understand what you say?

5. Do you have many misunderstandings? If so, name some recent disagreements. Did you cause them?

6. How do people view you? Do they like you? Respect you? Trust you?

You do not have to answer all the questions. Select those to which you can easily relate and that you feel will help you uncover the real you. Your responses to the sentence completion blanks in Journal Exercise 1 will provide additional data from your experiences.

THE SELF I'D LIKE TO BE   The imagined self is both what you would really like to be and how you hope others view you. It is easy to think or daydream about what you would really like to be, but how do you go about creating this mythical, beautiful, intelligent, adventuresome, and unique person in your daily routine? The first thing you do is find a mask or role that allows you to exercise this freedom. We have all, at times, been involved in a "put-on." How many times have you wanted to speak with a foreign accent, draw attention to yourself, or just come out of your shell? Now that you have

started realizing that there are many facets of yourself, and have started analyzing them, do you find some areas of your personality a put-on intended to fool people—possibly even yourself? Have you found that if you assume a role or mask, you do not get hurt as easily?

An example of combining a role and a mask concerns someone preparing for a raft trip down the Colorado River. Bruce began practicing his British accent, grew a mustache, and developed the vocabulary to impress people on the trip. When he reached the base and began packing the raft, an Englishman stepped forward as the guide and Bruce and his put-on were put out.

No one really wants to be exposed as a fraud. But you run this risk daily when you insist on hiding behind a mask or a role. How many people do you know who would be lost without their roles? For example, does your boss know how to act with employees away from the factory or the office? Or, is an authoritarian role still present? Some people can change "hats" and still be the same person in each role. Many times your friends may think you are an understanding and good listener, but does the brother, sister, or spouse who shares a room with you feel the same way?

It is natural for all of us to want to be something different from the individuals we perceive ourselves to be. But we must be cautious about the masks and roles we put on to hide our emotions and feelings. Maybe we are soft and sensitive on the inside, but to avoid being taken advantage of, we don a facade of coolness or hardness that keeps people away. Sometimes our imagined self is an individual who desires to be loved and to love others, but we wonder how we can become more like this ideal self.

Sidney Jourard states that "a choice that confronts everyone at every moment is this: Shall we permit our fellows to know us as we now are, or shall we remain enigmas, wishing to be seen as persons we are not?"[5] He further contends that we have always had the choice of being honest, but we have chosen to conceal our authenticity behind masks. We do this because we assume that others are hiding or misrepresenting their real feelings and intentions. We use this camouflaging process to protect ourselves from criticism and rejection. When we have not honestly presented ourselves to others, we are misunderstood. This misunderstanding leads to breakdowns in communication, and to frustration and rejection. Yet, according to Jourard, authenticity can be dangerous. After all, we're all that we have, and if we lay ourselves bare, what will happen next? However, studies have proven that when we become honest with others, for the most part they reflect this process and become honest with us.[6]

You can change if you want to; you can be yourself with people. You have to start with those you love and who love you in return. Then you can work your way up to your most unlikely and unyielding prospect. For instance, a young man named Bob was concerned about his next-door neighbor Jack, the most difficult person he had known. The final project in his speech communication course recommended that he deal with his most difficult human relations problem on a one-to-one basis. This process included using what he had learned in intrapersonal and interpersonal communication. Bob's next-door neighbor was always causing him trouble. Whenever Bob tried to be friendly by saying, "Good morning," Jack would retort, "What's good about it?" Jack burned his trash whenever Bob and his family cooked outside on the grill, and he deliberately parked in front of Bob's driveway. He was a nuisance.

But Bob had been working on being honest with those close to him, and he had decided that it was time to start working with the more difficult individuals in his life. He could test Carl Rogers's statement, "when I accept others as they are, they change." Accepting his neighbor would be a tremendous feat.

One day Jack's car rolled down his drive and smashed through the end of his garage. Bob decided to go next door and use his carpentry skills to help Jack repair the damage. Bob was nervous about offering, but he felt that he needed to extend himself. He went next door, and Jack opened the door and said, "Well, what do you want?" Bob was ready to take his tools and go home. But for the sake of the course, Carl Rogers, and his own self-concept, he said, "Listen, Jack, I know you need help on your garage. Let's tackle it together, and it will be done in no time." Jack backed off, somewhat surprised, and invited Bob in. While Bob worked with Jack, he

[5] Sidney M. Jourard, The Transparent Self, 2d ed. (New York: Van Nostrand Reinhold Books, 1971), p. vii.
[6] Ibid.

learned that Jack's last home had burned to the ground because of Jack's careless smoking habits. Jack and his family had escaped with minor injuries, but they had lost everything. Bob began to realize what Jack must be going through; as a result of being honest with each other, their communication improved, and they established a basis for a growing relationship.

Another example is recorded in Jess Lair's "*I Ain't Much, Baby—But I'm All I've Got.*" Sherry, a student, was having difficulties with a grouchy widow neighbor. Remembering that her neighbor's birthday was on Sunday, Sherry thought, "Maybe I don't really understand her. I know, I'll bake a cake and let my husband take it down to her—that way if she barks too loud I won't get hurt. Stop! You stupid fool you—I must understand the reason why I decided to make this act of graciousness. Be yourself and put all your effort into it."

On Sunday she took the cake that she had baked and knocked on the neighbor's door. The door opened and the woman barked, "Well . . . what do you want?" Sherry handed the cake to the woman and said, "Happy birthday." The woman's face softened, and she invited Sherry in. Sherry noticed that the woman had pictures of her husband and children on every table and wall. As the neighbor cut the cake, she said, "You know, Sherry, you look quite a bit like my daughter." She then explained that her husband and sons had been killed in an automobile accident and that her daughter was badly scarred. She blamed herself because she had insisted that they take a trip East, and the rest of the family had gone along just for her. Sherry realized that she had given this woman a chance to talk with her and not just at her; the communication affected both of their self-concepts.[7]

> *To grow is to change, and to have changed*
> *often is to have grown much.*
>
> —*John Henry Newman*

Many people would feel uncomfortable if their friends knew their problems or fears. If your friends knew your fears, they could possibly help you resolve them. Would you be afraid to tell your friends? How many of you would tell anyone that you are afraid of the dark? At some point everyone has been alone at night and has heard sounds that would seem natural if others were at home; but when you are alone, the sounds become foreign and can be a source of fear. If you discuss the situation, it may become less frightening. When you learn that others also have or have had these fears, you understand that your fears can be conquered.

Exercise 4

Fear Disclosure

The entire class may sit comfortably in a circle or break into smaller groups of five to seven people. Someone should begin by sharing a fear with the group; then members of the group should discuss whether or not they share the problem or share ways of conquering the fear. For example, one student revealed

---

[7] Jess Lair, "*I Ain't Much, Baby—But I'm All I've Got*" (New York: Doubleday, 1969), pp. 18 and 19.

that she was afraid of groups and especially of self-disclosure. Others in the group shared this fear and commiserated with her, while still others saw definite worth in being open and sharing their thoughts. The members of the group found that communication channels were being opened and that they were learning to think about the others in a communicative situation. There were also those who felt insecure about success in life and who expressed what they had done or were doing to handle the problem.

This exercise is not a cure-all for the fears one has, but it does offer exposure to honest communication. You may work with this exercise as long as you feel comfortable and have time. Be aware that it will take time in some instances to share openly.

THE SELF OTHERS THINK I AM

One of the greatest hurdles you face in understanding self-concept evolves from what you think others feel about you. After you have handled how you perceive yourself and have searched your mental attic for your ideal self, the next problem to consider is your idea of how others see you. This picture can be, and usually is, quite unnerving. You perceive how people feel about you through their verbal and nonverbal actions. If you say, "Hello," to the girl at the next desk and she doesn't respond, it can damage your ego. You might think, "What's the matter, doesn't she like me?" Possibly she didn't hear you, but you are already developing an "I'm a zero" complex.

Being ignored is perhaps one of the most threatening reactions you can face. You want to get along with others, gain approval, and feel a sense of belonging. Yet you would rather be abused than ignored. You learn in part to accept the abuse. Your parents may have told you that you are not as humorous as your brother or as cute as your sister. Schoolteachers have suggested that you are not the smartest member of your family. The basketball coach says that you are not tall enough. The drama teacher adds that you are not talented enough for the lead. All these experiences lead you to a depressing view of how the world perceives you, and you internalize the reactions of others as part of your self-concept. On the other hand, you may be the humorous brother or the good-looking sister, the tall, four-letter man that girls swoon over, or the intelligent and sensitive actress ready for Broadway. The accolades you draw from the crowd have reinforced your self-concept.

Most of us, however, lie somewhere between the doldrums of depression and the super "high" of social acceptance. We are aware that some of the people surrounding us communicate an unspoken acceptance or rejection, and we look for the positive and negative cues that others give off.

It is important to examine how you feel others think about you, and even to ask a select few whether they really view you as awkward or unfriendly. Many times what they said in anger or haste was not meant to be a personal affront; but you accept it as such. Consider Pam's experience. She was a good student in the Air Force language school, with a B average. After her training, she received a permanent-duty assignment. During the first week of duty at her new assignment, the workload of the veteran linguists was very heavy, and none were free to supervise on-the-job training for Pam and the other new linguists just arriving at the station. In fact, the workload was so heavy that Pam and the others were put to work by themselves, without supervision and help. Pam was given some "routine" work—routine at least, to the veteran linguists. But it seemed quite hard for Pam. She did a poor job of interpreting the material and made some crucial mistakes. Her supervisor noticed the mistakes; hoping to make Pam try harder and do better work, he began cutting Pam down in front of all the others. The supervisor told her that she was no good, that she was completely incompetent, and that she would never make a good linguist if she could not even handle the routine material without completely fouling up. All in all, he told Pam that she was just no good at the job. Weeks passed; as the workload lessened, Pam and the other new linguists were put in an on-the-job training program. During and after the program, Pam was very tense. She could not relax and concentrate on her work. She was always afraid that she was going to make a mistake. As other trainees began to receive some of the more complicated materials, Pam kept slipping further and further behind, just because she was afraid that she couldn't handle the material. Pam remained a poor linguist not because she was incompetent or ignorant of the foreign language, but because she lacked confidence in herself. She was always sure she would fail. Consequently, she was only allowed to work on the unimportant material, and she spent most of her time as a "go-for," going for coffee, sandwiches, and paper supplies.

A second example demonstrates the importance of carefully assessing the comments of others that you internalize as your self-concept. When he was just a little boy, José's father told him—in a joking manner—that he was not worth a nickel, and his brother told him that he was ugly. For most of his young adult life, these statements affected his self-confidence. He was shy in his interpersonal relations because he felt worthless and unattractive. He had to prove to himself that his family had incorrectly judged his worth. Today he is a debonair man in his sixties, a wise and loving contributor to the world around him. He knows this and is appreciated by his friends and acquaintances. Most important, he finally learned not to accept any hasty statement from another as a part of his self-concept, and he shares his experience with others struggling with negative criticism.

Criticism has its place if it is pointing out valid flaws or problems that you should correct. But how frequently do you allow this negative criticism to be a part of your self-concept, so that you see yourself as a useless or worthless being? You must consider what is valid and what is not. No one is perfect, but you should strive for understanding and acceptance of yourself. You need to develop a strong and stable self-concept to serve as a buffer against negative criticism.

You also need to be careful about what you accept of others' judgments. How often do you live up to the negative qualities others project on you? Ask yourself, "So what if I know what another person thinks about me? Those thoughts are not what I am." If you had a dream that a tiger attacked and viciously mauled you, would you get a bandage when you woke up? Of course not! Other people's thoughts about you are no more powerful than that tiger unless you mentally accept them and make them your own. If others say malicious things about you, it is going to hurt, but you do not have to accept what they say. Isn't it comforting to realize that your thinking about yourself cannot be damaged by others unless you allow it? As Abraham Lincoln once said, "It is difficult to make a man miserable while he feels he is worthy of himself and claims kindred to the great God who made him."

THE SELF I
THINK
AND ACT

The self that emerges from your awareness of your physical and mental competencies supplies a framework for your attitudes, beliefs, and values. If the self you believe in has two left feet, you will rule out dancing and possibly deny yourself a congenial walk around the block. As you realize what your body can do, you develop aspects of your self-concept. For example, if you are an athlete, you know how many lengths of the pool you can swim and how many laps around the track you can run. You perceive yourself as physically fit, strong, and toned.

Mental competencies operate in much the same manner. Poor high school grades or standardized test scores that suggest minimal intelligence may have deceived you; yet you know you can perform well in class or on the job. You should be concerned with using your physical and mental abilities to prove things to yourself rather than to others. What do you know about your physical and mental competencies?

Exercise 5

Mental and
Physical
Competencies

As an individual exercise, in the left-hand column list your physical competencies, and in the right-hand column list your mental competencies.

Physical
competencies

Mental
competencies

Now compare the two. Have you missed anything? For example, Gene perceives his physical competencies in terms of his height, agility, and athletic prowess. He plays center for the college basketball team and is six feet nine inches tall. He states that he is alert on the basketball court, but that he has difficulty listening to lectures on chemistry and world history. However, he is a whiz in math. These competencies suggest something about his self-concept: he is in a position to put his competencies to work for him.

On the other hand, Kay believes that she has few competencies. She is an average student and perceives her mental competencies as an honest caring for others and an ability to discern problems. She feels that her physical competencies are weak—she can see, hear, smell, taste, touch, and walk. She has more to offer than she can see at this level. Possibly she should evaluate her attitudes, beliefs, and values.

Your attitudes, beliefs, and values shape your personality and establish guidelines for your behavior. Attitudes are your predispositions toward a person or thing—positive or negative. You acquire and develop them throughout your life. A belief is the acceptance of a specific proposition, and it is socially determined and based on personal experience. Combined attitudes and beliefs are shaped by individual family, religious, and educational backgrounds. However, attitudes and beliefs differ in intensity and desirability. Finally, a value is anything of worth. Values, then, are the goods of life: in the Hebrew-Christian culture they can be traced to the Ten Commandments, the seven virtues, and the seven mortal sins.[8]

The following example shows how the three operate together. You may have an attitude of religious tolerance, but you believe specifically in Judaism and value the Decalogue. For another example, you may have a negative attitude toward capital punishment because you value the right to live, even though you believe specifically in rehabilitation and imprisonment for crimes of homicide.

It should now be evident how attitudes, beliefs, and values help to shape your world. In this next exercise we ask you to take account of your attitudes, beliefs, and values, and see whether they enhance your conscious worth.

Exercise 6

Value, Belief, and Attitude Identification

List five things you value, five beliefs you hold dear, and five attitudes you have about your life.

Values

---

[8] Virgil L. Baker, "The Role of Human Values in Communication," in *Communication Probes* by Brent D. Peterson, Gerald M. Goldhaber, and R. Wayne Pace (Chicago: Science Research Associates, 1974), p. 6.

Beliefs

Attitudes

Explain how your physical and mental competencies enter into your values, beliefs, and attitudes.

Now try filling out Journal Exercise 2 at the back of the book in light of what you are learning about yourself.

You can use the following group exercises in place of others or in addition to the ones already provided in this chapter.

Exercise 7

Values and Objects

What gives an object worth? How many times have you seen people go to junk yards, garage sales, antique shows, and auctions to buy things that you feel are junk? Has a parent, spouse, or someone else in your life ever questioned the value of something that you purchased? A man's old work clothes could very well be his prized possessions. How many of you have clung to an old pair of sneakers? What do you think gives an object value?

1. Make a list of possessions that you value.

2. Rank this list by calling your most valued treasure number one, the next number two, and so on.

3. Now make ten copies of your list of objects.

4. Give the copies to ten different people and have them rank the objects in the order of the objects' values for them.

5. Compare your order with that of the others.

6. Where do they differ? Why do you feel your objects mean more to you than to someone else?

Exercise 8

Wallet Identification

Select a partner and exchange wallets. In five to ten minutes prepare an introduction of this person for the class based solely on the information you found in the wallet. See how much information you can find out about this person.

1. What kind of a person do you find?

2. How old?

3. How tall?

4. To what organizations does your partner belong?

5. Do you find credit cards?

6. Are there family pictures?

7. What judgments can you make about your partner?

==

==

Exercise 9

Self-Presentation

The goal of this exercise is to express verbally and nonverbally the unique characteristics that make up your self-concept. You may make this speech as a formal presentation to the class or as an exercise in sharing in small groups.

Suggestions for Verbal Material

1. Examine how you perceive yourself; share these discovered traits with your classmates.

2. Answer these questions: Do you view yourself as an aggressive, honest, and happy person? Or do you see yourself as a shy and unhappy individual? Do you try to hide your real self? (The sentence completion blanks in Journal Exercise 1 will help you view yourself.)

3. Try to include the significant experiences or personalities you have encountered—both the successes and the failures.

4. Present your most strongly held beliefs—and the causes for which you would work.

5. You might even consider discussing the problems or barriers that you encounter in communicating with others.

6. Limit yourself to a three- to five-minute presentation.

Suggestions for Nonverbal Material

If you want to maintain audience interest and attention, you will find that it is more effective to use many communication channels than to rely on just one. Some techniques that other speech students have used in answering the above questions include collages, pantomime, and music. The collages can consist of a flat poster of words, pictures, or both. Many interesting collages, however, have been drawn or painted on objects that students believe represent their "true"

selves. One student who felt that she did nothing but play roles to suit other people cut a plastic wig-head in half, hinged it, and designed the inside to represent her "real" ideas and the outside to represent the way she communicated her thoughts to others. A man who saw himself as buried deep inside many roles brought many boxes, one fitted inside another, all designed differently. Another student brought in a plant because she could not represent herself in nonliving form. The roots gave a sense of family attachment, and the leaves suggested a reaching out to touch others. A young man kept changing hats to symbolize his role progression. He started out with a Cub Scout beanie and ended with a hard hat representing his present job. We aren't calling for a "true confession" here, but if you supply only a superficial view of yourself, that's the self others will come to know.

EVALUATION OF INTRA-PERSONAL SELF-PRESENTATION

Analyze the strengths and weaknesses of your presentation for Exercise 9 by describing and evaluating your communication behavior in the following areas:

1. *Preparation:* What goals did you set for this presentation? How did you select your material? How did you practice the speech?
2. *Presentation:* What factors in your setting affected your presentation? Were you aware of tension in your speech, of audience responses, or of other environmental factors?
3. *Evaluation:* Did your efforts meet your expectations? What do you think you did particularly well? How well did you handle your collage or other nonverbal material? What do you need to work toward in your next assignment?

4. *Re-presentation*: Assume that you are going to repeat this assignment. Judging from your first attempt, what aspects of your preparation or presentation will you change so that you can better meet your goals?

SUMMARY   Intrapersonal communication is the center of all communication. Since communication takes place within you as either a sender or a receiver, it is important for you to understand your self-concept. How you view yourself depends largely on how you interpret and send messages. You first need to understand and accept your "real" self; because you are in a state of becoming, you are constantly changing. Thus self-disclosure is an ongoing activity that results in better interpersonal communication and that gives you an opportunity to learn how others see themselves. It is vital to your development of intrapersonal communication that you listen to others describe their perceptions of themselves. You may soon learn that your self-concept is similar to others, and you may learn how to be more honest—no longer needing to wear masks or to camouflage your true self.

You need to be careful about what you accept from others' judgments. Others can't damage your thinking about yourself unless you let it happen. Therefore, you should be able to examine your physical and mental competencies realistically and be able to accept yourself.

What do you know of yourself? You should be aware of (1) how you view yourself, (2) how you define your ideal self, (3) how you feel others view you, and (4) how your physical and mental competencies shape your attitudes, beliefs, and values. Self-concept and self-disclosure are important to your growth. You should start thinking about the positive ways in which you can use self-concept and about why self-concept is important to total communication.

SUPPLEMENTARY READING

In the selection that follows, James W. Felt explores the importance of discarding facades and masks that hide the "real" you, and he discusses the importance of wanting to be yourself. Do you want to be yourself? After you read this article think about how it affected you and whether you changed your answer to that question.

HOW TO BE YOURSELF

JAMES W. FELT

"Be yourself!" Psychologists urge this upon us. Philosophers stress it. We increasingly recognize that it is profoundly necessary. But just what does it *mean* to "be yourself"?

In a sense this is a large question, and so I want to focus on just one sense in which I think "Be yourself" is often *mis*understood. I attack such a mis-interpretation, of course, on the basis of what I believe to be an essential ingredient in what it does mean to "be yourself."

If there is anything we do with relish and at every available opportunity it is make *things* out of *events*. When there is flashing we make a thing out of it and call it "lightning." When we get a shock we say there is "electricity" in the wire. When everything has been shaking we say, "That was an earthquake," just as we might, in another context, say, "That was an elephant." And this is natural for us, because things are not only easier to deal with than events, they are also easier to talk about. Both the language and the logic we inherit from the Greeks put a premium on the fixed, on the changeless, on *things*.

And so both psychotherapists and their patients spontaneously talk of "discarding masks," of "peeling off layers," of "uncovering the real self," as one would uncover the body by disrobing it. The question is, what can this "real self" signify?

When I "discard a false self" I am obviously not throwing away some *thing* as I would a gum wrapper: I am ceasing to live my life in an unauthentic way. What right, then, do I have to suppose that there is a "true self" waiting to be found under these "masks," as I would expect to find my foot if I took off my sock? But suppose that there is such a "myself" which I am to "be." Suppose, in other words, to "be yourself" means to "live up to your true self (which is already latent within you)." Then what is the nature of that self? The unspoken assumption seems to be that this "true self" was given from eternity or at least from conception, that it has a definite character, that it is just waiting to be filled out, as the acorn is waiting to turn into the oak. My problem in this case is simply to discover, to uncover, my "true self" so that I can live up to it.

Such a view is not far from the Greek idea of fate. We find something like this, I think, in Hermann Hesse's famous novel *Demian.* Its appeal to youth surely lies in its "Be yourself" theme. Hesse himself places on the title page of his work the following lines from its text: "I wanted only to live in accord with the promptings which came from my true self. Why was that so very difficult?"

But at the same time this true self of Hesse's is the self of fate:

"At this point a sharp realization burned within me: each man has his 'function' but none which he can choose himself, define, or perform as he pleases. . . . An enlightened man had but one duty—to seek the way to himself. . . . He might end up as poet or madman, as prophet or criminal—that was not his affair, ultimately it was of no concern. His task was to discover his own destiny—not an arbitrary one—and live it out wholly and resolutely within himself" (Bantam edition, pp. 107–8).

The ideal that Hesse holds up for us is the man who "seeks nothing but his own fate," the man who "only seeks his destiny."

But if, on the contrary, "Be yourself" means simply "Live authentically," then what sort of self is the object of this exhortation? There is just plain old me, the product of all my past experiences, my physical and mental limitations, above all of my past decisions. But this me is never settled nor is it prefabricated. It is always on the way, always in the process of self-creation. At every moment I am creating the me that I choose to be: there is nothing fated here. Whatever my limitations, whatever my past, I hold this me in my hands at every moment, to fashion as I will. Bergson claims we have an immediate experience, if we would only recognize it, "of being creators of our intentions, of our decisions, of our acts, and by that, of our habits, our characters, ourselves." To be myself, then, does not amount to uncovering the sort of me that I was born or fated to be. It means discovering my own true freedom to fashion myself as I can and as I will.

In that sense psychotherapy may often leave off where it should begin. To discover *how* I am the product of my past only fills in the details of the obvious generalization that of course I *am* the product of my past. What I need at this point is to realize that, notwithstanding these limitations of the past, to learn to be myself means precisely to discover that I am in fact free to create my ever-emerging self on my own and in my own way.

If, then, I understand "Be yourself" to mean, "Uncover and live up to that destined self latent in you," I either chain myself to whatever image I evoke of this self, or else I abandon all responsibility for my actions on the grounds that what I do spontaneously lives up automatically to the demands of this hidden true self. But if I am skeptical of the existence of such a prefabricated self, if I take "Be yourself" to mean, "Live authentically, according to values as you yourself grasp them," then I am thrown onto my own responsibility about my life. My fate then consists precisely in the formation of that self which I myself create with every new decision of my freedom. It is I who at every moment decide what sort of man I shall be, and this is my human dignity. To be myself is to be free.

ADDITIONAL READING

Applbaum, Ronald L., et al. *Fundamental Concepts in Human Communication.* San Francisco: Canfield Press, 1973.
> A text that covers the fundamentals and handles all phases of the behavioral approach to speech communication. It provides supportive exercises and examples of models.

Cole, Jim. *The Facade.* Greeley, Colo.: Jim Cole, 1970.
> A picture book of the struggle to remove facades. It visually examines the problems of self-examination.

Johnson, David W. *Reaching Out.* Englewood Cliffs, N.J.: Prentice-Hall, 1972.
> An interpersonal how-to-do-it book in workbook form, with stimulating exercises for improving your interpersonal relationships. It incorporates the theory of both intrapersonal and interpersonal communication in an understandable fashion.

Lair, Jess. *"I Ain't Much, Baby—But I'm All I've Got."* Garden City, N.Y.: Doubleday, 1969.
> An autobiographical account of Lair's recovery from a heart attack, with Lair's realization that there is more to life than the hectic rat race. He shares the intrapersonal flavor of his psychology classes and the sense of the importance of self-awareness and self-esteem.

May, Rollo. *Man's Search For Himself.* New York: Signet Books, 1953.
> An examination of everyday anxieties, including the struggle to become a person and to undergo self-examination. It explains the strengths and weaknesses of knowing one's self.

Myers, Gail E., and Michele T. Myers. *The Dynamics of Human Communication.* New York: McGraw-Hill, 1973.
> A laboratory approach to understanding human communication, with materials on perception, language, and intrapersonal and interpersonal communication. The exercises provide stimulus situations for using the principles of human interaction rather than those of public speaking.

Powell, John. *Why Am I Afraid To Tell You Who I Am?* Niles, Ill.: Argus Communications, 1969.
> A book that discusses the difficulties of growing as a person and learning to cope with emotions, moods, and who you think you are. It shares the author's insights into self-awareness, self-discovery, growth, and communication, and it explores nearly forty games, roles, and masks.

Rogers, Carl. *On Becoming A Person.* Boston: Houghton Mifflin, 1961.
> An examination of how people become people. Rogers handles the question of how self-esteem and self-motivation relate to our understanding of self-concept in the process of becoming ourselves.

Sereno, Kenneth K., and Edward M. Bodaken. *Trans-Per: Understanding Human Communication.* Boston: Houghton Mifflin, 1975.
> An introductory textbook that uses a transactional-perceptual approach to human communication. Chapter seven surveys communication in the intrapersonal context through the book's original model, Trans-Per.

Wenburg, John R., and William W. Wilmot. *The Personal Communication Process.* New York: John Wiley & Sons, 1973.
> An introductory textbook discussing human communication as a behavioral science, with examples and supportive exercises. It explains the scientific methodology and theory used in developing intrapersonal and interpersonal communication.

There is an inevitable divergence, attributable to the imperfections of the human mind, between the world as it is and the world as men perceive it.

—*J. William Fulbright*

2. INDIVIDUAL PERCEPTION

OBJECTIVES   In this chapter we ask you to do the following:

1. Recognize how your senses distort reality.

2. Describe how you selectively perceive objects and people.

3. Understand that perception is a learned process.

4. Select ways of improving your perception of reality.

Where do you live? What is your family background? Are you black, yellow, or white? Are you privileged or underprivileged, intelligent or unintelligent? Would the answers to these questions tell you about your fundamental sense of self and your reason for being? They probably would not. Most people experience a need to find a meaning in life. Some people explore this need through a search for spiritual values. Others, hoping to establish their individuality, escape to a world of physical sensation by experimenting with drugs. Still others persuade themselves that they are "identifying" by getting heavily involved with groups or family relationships. You can see from these examples that people yearn to prove their worth as individuals.

You can satisfy the deep human longing for identification by realizing that you can do something about it. The need to escape from a computer age in which people are coldly categorized should not lead you to look for your individuality outside yourself—it should make you look inward and ask, "Who am I?"

This questioning process relies on whether you think of yourself as yellow, red, or purple, privileged or underprivileged, and so on. Perception is your experience of sensing, imagining, interpreting, and understanding the world. Behavioral scientists have used the term *perception* to mean those processes by which you become aware of the world around you and give it meaning. But no universal theory of perception exists. Your senses inform you that in the "real" world there are objects such as people, animals, houses, and flowers. Conventionally, all you know of this external world is what you can see, hear, smell, taste, and touch. However, recent studies in extrasensory perception, psychokinetics, and biofeedback suggest that there is more to perception than what you perceive through the five physical senses. This book cannot begin to touch on such areas, but it recognizes that empirical research is being done and that ESP, psychokinetics, biofeedback, and other areas cannot be ignored. For practical reasons, we are confining our remarks on perception to the five physical senses.

DISTORTION OF REALITY

The senses predominate in perceptual experience. Have you ever been fooled into seeing water on the highway on a hot sunny day or into seeing train tracks that look narrower at a distance? Just because you cannot hear dog whistles or see X-rays, radio waves, and infrared lighting, are they nonexistent? You are somewhat limited in your processing of certain stimuli if you can't relate them to anything in your perceptual storehouse. You modify the experiences that you perceive through your senses to fit your needs and expectations.

Do you ever remember playing the game of haunted house at a Halloween party? You were blindfolded, taken into a room, and told that you would feel a bowl filled with eyeballs. They were really peeled grapes, but they certainly felt like eyeballs when you couldn't see them. The warm spaghetti felt like worms and even tasted like them when you were forced to feel and eat some. The apple you had to eat tasted like an onion because the onion was held right underneath your nose. The clanking of chains, rolling of marbles, and blowing of a fan convinced you that something, someone, or even a spirit had to be in that room. When you were finally unmasked, there you were staring at yourself in a mirror. You may have screamed in terror, like most adolescents who go through a "horror house." This familiar example of junior high school fun shows that you cannot really trust your senses to inform you about a situation.

Exercise 10

Sensory Awareness Inventory

How in touch are you with your senses? Your past experiences inform you that the sky is blue, skunks have an unpleasant odor, and hot objects are uncomfortable to touch. But what happens when you try to extend what appear to be the normal limits of your senses? Try to answer the following questions:

1. What color is today?

2. What color is the smell of your favorite perfume?

3. How high is the sky? What does the sky sound like?

4. What does your favorite day taste like?

5. What color is a hug?

6. What does a favorite song or work of music smell like? How would you describe its shape?

7. What does yellow taste like?

8. What color is the sound of a parade?

9. How would you describe the texture of your own name?

10. What would your eyes feel like if they could shake hands?

11. What does your favorite season sound and smell like?

12. What is your favorite sense?

13. What smell describes your self-concept?

14. What color is love?

15. Write whatever enters your head (in two or three sentences).

Have you ever thought of extending your senses in this way? Were the questions difficult to answer? If so, why? This exercise may seem unusual because you seldom need to extend your senses. However, many people must learn to perceive common phenomena by different sensory means. Consider the deaf person who learns language by visual and tactile associations and who communicates with others by reading sign language. You can share ideas and experiences and make decisions without making or hearing a sound. Likewise, the blind person may "know" what objects look like by using sounds, odors, and tactile experience. Extending your senses may teach you to perceive the ideas and values of others in a broader sense: it might teach you to be more understanding and open to all perceptions.

On the other hand, you can probably think of situations in which your senses have been deceived. For example, eyes are fascinating mechanisms. The light rays reflected from objects you focus on are fixed on a three-eighth inch spot on the back walls of your eyes. The stimuli are changed into electrical impulses that affect the nervous system; in turn, you mentally process the impulses negatively or positively according to past experience and act or react accordingly.[1] Both physically and mentally, the externalized object becomes an internalized experience. Because light rays bounce off the walls of your eyes differently from the way they would in anyone else, you have a unique experience. It is impossible to get inside other people's heads to see the world as they do and to see why they act or react as they do. So keep in mind that the senses can deceive. But also remember that they are about all that you have.

The following two examples are true experiences involving the senses and individualized perceptions. The first situation explains why expectations sometimes cause you to see reality as dull and uninteresting.

Traveling across the Arizona desert on a train, someone observed two young adults talking about the boredom of the desert. They felt that it was nothing but "hot, flat land." A gentleman sitting nearby was listening to their complaints about the dullness of the landscape. Suddenly he leaned over and spoke to them.

[1] Don Fabun, *Communication: The Transfer of Meaning* (Beverly Hills, Calif.: Glencoe Press, 1968), p. 9.

"Do you see that band of purple, yellow, and white in the distance?" They looked and saw a thin line of mixed colors. "Those are desert flowers hugging the sand to escape the wind," he said. "Look at the oddly shaped cactus trees." He explained how that species flowered and described how large the trees could grow. "Watch the hills over there; now they are blue, soon they will turn rose, then purple as the sun goes down."

As he talked to these two people, the desert changed their feelings from boredom and disinterest to interest and appreciation. What happened? The desert had not changed, but their impression of it had. Willingness to accept a helpful word, even a rebuke, can change a person's concept of things. Such willingness is often essential to make progress.

Frequently we neglect to extend or expand our perceptions, casually seeing or hearing something and assigning it meaning without clearly perceiving it. This second situation demonstrates that we need to examine what we see more closely.

One hot summer night an art student was trying to cool off in front of the fan in her dormitory room. She received a phone call and drew some bugs on a piece of paper while she was talking. Later that evening, when she returned to her room, she saw a line of bugs crawling on her desk. For a couple of minutes she swatted the intruders—first with a broom, then a fly swatter, and finally her shoe. When she got close enough with her shoe, she realized that the fan had blown her doodlings of bugs and had made them appear very real. Later it was something she could laugh about; but at the time, she pondered it, realizing that she had been taken in by her five senses. For a brief moment she had actually tried to kill some bugs because she saw little insects crawling on her desk. Her sense of vision gave life to her scrawls.

The five material senses make things appear real. Camera angles would call a ball player safe when, in actuality, he was out if you viewed him from a closer vantage point. The horizon line makes you feel that you will fall off the edge of the world, and that small speck of machinery flying in the sky seats two hundred adults comfortably. Although your vision might discredit the validity of these things, your experience assures you of their reliability.

PERCEPTION AND MEANING

A common ground for understanding perception is perceptual structure. Our environment is what we perceive it to be. We can view it as pleasant, good, happy, relaxing, rewarding, intolerable, catastrophically wretched, and so on.

We all structure our perceptions. We selectively view objects, people, events, and words and give them meaning; it is our meaning, but it is meaning nevertheless. For example, if an instructor asked students to bring a blue triangle to class, each individual would probably bring in a personal concept of blue—sky blue, dark blue, royal blue, midnight blue, turquoise blue, baby blue. The instructor might even get some equilateral, obtuse, acute, scalene, right angle, and isosceles triangles.

In our classes, students brought in triangles of different colors, sizes, and shapes. The following examples show what some students perceived a blue triangle to mean: a depressed triangle filled with tears, a poem about love as a blue triangle, a short story, and a slip of paper with the words *a blue triangle* written on it. Each individual brought in a perception of a blue triangle. We observed that all of our perceptions are different and that our use of language affects our perceptions.

Jane, a teacher who had recently moved to an industrial city, wrote the symbols *CAT* on the blackboard and then asked the students what they thought the symbols suggested. They replied in unison, "Caterpillar." Momentarily, she thought she was in a cultural wilderness. Her students quickly informed her that the city was the national headquarters for Caterpillar Tractor Company, and that there were five local plants. She perceived the word *cat* to mean an animal, and so she assumed that her students would be recalling their own experiences with a household pet, not associating the word with a place of employment.

You selectively perceive according to your past experiences and knowledge. If you were asked to describe an object or an incident in the past, your description would depend on how you perceived that object and situation and what you remembered about it. Unless you were sure of what you saw, your recollection of what actually happened and who was involved could be distorted.

For instance, if you saw a man walk out of Joe's Tavern carrying two wrapped, cylindrical packages under each arm, you might perceive that this man had two bottles of liquor in the bags because they were twisted at the top and because he walked out of the tavern with them. This scene might shock you, since this man is your minister and he shuns the use of alcohol. When you describe this situation to someone else, do you consider the facts—if, indeed, there are any? Will you slander your minister through your description? Suppose that you are wrong. Luckily, you happen to call someone who knows that Joe's Tavern sells the best cold cuts in town and that your minister just purchased salami and bologna for the youth group's picnic on Saturday. Was your perception incorrect? How can you avoid these mistakes? One way to minimize some of the horror of mistaken perception is to be aware that you are fallible. Also remember that perception is individual and implies that you have attached meaning to a situation. Because you are a unique individual and have created your own world, you perceive the real world in your own way.

LEARNING PERCEPTION Because we have been educated to structure and categorize our experiences, we selectively perceive a situation based on past experience. In a sense, we select what we want from the world. We also narrow our perceptions based on our decisions. If we only look out the east windows of our home, our experience will be narrow. Remember that selective perception for the most part deals with what we have been taught to see, hear, smell, taste, and touch. Our experience teaches us about the people and objects within our environment. Through successive experiences with cats, we expect to see cats that have four feet, one tail, and fluffy hair. Through experiences we also learn that when a cat is frightened it arches its back and its hair stands on end. If it went bow-wow instead of meow, we might be concerned that something was indeed different about this animal.

We hope that in understanding your self-concept you will extend your selective perception so that you want and learn to perceive more. You must want to stop viewing life through one dimension; you must look at all sides of an issue, not just the ones with which you are comfortable or that fit your perceptual structure. It is time to expand your perceptions of yourself and of others.

You have been taught to process through structure and classification the infinite number of stimuli bombarding you. English teachers return themes, saying that they lack structure and organization. But the problem may be that your perceptions and those of your instructor differ. (This, however, does not mean that one of you may not be wrong.) You are educated to adopt accepted rules of organization in order to communicate more clearly with others.

While we see things in different ways, we all have something in common in our individuality. We have learned to classify things in terms of size, shape, density, texture, and so on. In the story of *Goldilocks and the Three Bears*, we are able to perceive Goldilocks's world because we have made similar classifications. "The porridge is too hot." "The chair is too soft." "The bed is just right." Our perceptions give structure to our world. We perceive people to be of a certain height and weight, and we mentally see them as tall, fat, short, or thin. When we see the head of Johnny Carson on television, six inches from the floor, we have mentally perceived that he does indeed have a body attached below his head—even though it is not growing through the floor. Why can we accept this bodiless picture of a man? Our past experience dictates that he is complete, and we subconsciously perceive him as a whole individual. Psychologists call this processing *closure*.

The gestalt principle of closure states that we subconsciously or consciously complete the uncompleted. Psychology texts show pictures of incomplete triangles and circles, and the mind naturally completes the picture. Advertising has taken advantage of the consumer through psychological gimmickry that plays on the individual's closure perception. For example, a Volkswagen ad some years ago showed a line of VW's going down the page, but the reader never saw a whole car—just mentally perceiving it as a whole. Another example is figure 2–1. In this ad the Volkswagen is incomplete, yet we actively perceive it as a whole.

Unlike our subconscious, we don't always visualize the whole. When we walk into a crowded room, we may selectively perceive only the faces of those we know and totally exclude the others. Our perception is affected by what is in our thoughts. If we stopped someone on the street to get directions to a local gas station and got the reply, "You go down a minute and then take a minute and a half until you come to a quarter of a second and then you turn at the next half minute," we would probably be confused. We would not be anticipating that kind of response. Communication effectiveness is enhanced when we adapt to each other's perceptual structures.

We associate a psychological set with every concept, idea, or thing; when other people deal with that concept, idea, or thing, we anticipate that they will deal with it essentially in the same psychological way.

Figure 2-1

For example, spell the word *spot* aloud. Now, what do you do when you come to a green light? If you answered, "Stop," you were conditioned by your previous perception of spelling the word *spot*. If this word game didn't work on you because you perceived the word visually, ask someone else to spell *spot*, see what their reaction is, and compare it with your own. You may wish to try another game. Spell the word *joke*. Now, what do you call the white of an egg—the yolk? No, the white of the egg is called the albumin.

You are somewhat limited in processing certain stimuli if you can't relate them to anything in your perceptual storehouse. You constantly modify your sensory experiences to fit your needs; you see what you expect to see. When you are looking for a phone booth, you are not likely to see a mail box, fire hydrant, or litter can because you are directing your attention to the phone booth. If you have driven to a movie, you expect when the picture is over to see your car where you parked it. It would be unnerving not to find it there.

You see what gratifies your needs. When you go to a restaurant, it is only natural to see what appeals to both your taste buds and your wallet. (Sometimes the latter never satisfies the former.) If you hear someone ordering veal Parmigiana, you might wonder where it is on the menu. It is actually just above the line where you are reading about the steak and surf. Your eye drifted to the steak and not the veal because the veal didn't gratify your need. Many people subscribe to *Playboy* or *Playgirl* because of this particular form of selective perception. What catches their eye?

Exercise 11

Perceptual Distortion

In this group excercise, observe the two perceptual pictures (figure 2–2 and figure 2–3). What do you see? List your initial responses under each picture. Now select one of the two and discuss whether the old man's face or the panda's head is really there. Can you teach or help someone to see either of these pictures? If the head and face are there, why did you have a difficult time seeing them? If you feel they are not there, what are those people who "see" them really seeing?

Figure 2-2
Can you find the face of the man?
Response:

Figure 2-3

Can you find the panda?
Response:

IMPROVING PERCEPTION

Up to this point, we have shown that your senses affect your perception and that you selectively perceive the world. You structure messages according to past experiences; you select—filter out—the stimuli you wish to process. With the full use of your faculties, you are still capable of misperceiving or misjudging what is going on around you. Many times your filtering system becomes clogged, and you discover that you are not aware of your environment, that you are spending more time tuning out than tuning in. Try checking this in your own experience. If you tune out people and events, ask yourself why; begin tuning in the world around you; observe other people, as well as your thoughts about them and yourself. Being conscious of what you are thinking is a good way to start. Knowing that you perceive experiences selectively, you should not be so impatient with others or yourself just because you view the world differently.

In this awakening process of understanding your self-concept, try to consider *why* you are the way you are now; you need to be critically aware of how you perceive your world. We have frequently asked you to think about yourself and your self-concept. Have you wondered why? Asking "Why?" is an important part of the process of perceptive questioning.

Asking questions about *how* you think and *why* you think is a part of critical thinking.

We want you to extend your critical thinking to critical self-awareness. Learning to perceive a situation analytically involves examining details. For example, a dollar bill has become just a piece of paper currency for most people. How many things can you observe about it? For example, how many "ones" can you find on it? Compare your total with that of other classmates. Now invent some of your own exercises, and share them with your class.

You should actively be attempting to learn more about the world and applying new ways of viewing a situation to the way you perceive your environment. If you can visualize a situation in one way, try to find two or more possible explanations so that you see it differently.

> *To listen to my intuition is to identify with my*
> *entire awareness, to be my entire experience, and not*
> *just my conscious perception. My total awareness*
> *synthesizes into a calm sense of direction that is*
> *above reason.*
> —*Hugh Prather*

Exercise 12

Perception

This group exercise and the three exercises that follow will help you develop a keener awareness of people and events. For the first exercise, break into groups of three or five. Observe each of the following pictures and write down your immediate response to them.

In the first picture, what do you perceive the woman to be doing? What is she thinking?

Photograph by Paul S. Conklin

Figure 2-4

Photograph by Paul S. Conklin

Figure 2-5

In the second picture, what is the boy doing? What is he thinking?

What are they doing together?

Photograph by Paul S. Conklin

Figure 2-6

Figure 2-7

What does the picture with the photographer suggest?

Compare your reactions with those of others in your group. Are your perceptions different? Why? Are your perceptions the same? If they are the same, talk to other groups to see whether their members' perceptions differed.

Look at the picture below. What is happening in it? What emotions does it express? Put yourself in that individual's place. What is going on in your thoughts? Share your comments with group members.

Photograph by Arthur Tress, Magnum Photos, Inc.

Figure 2-8

Exercise 14

**Perceptual
Communication
Skills**

This exercise is different from the others in this text because we include an actual situation that occurred while students were completing this exercise. We asked for four volunteers and asked three of them to leave the room. We asked the remaining student, Carol, to draw a picture on the board. Figure 2–9 shows her picture of the cartoon character Woody Woodpecker. We covered the picture and brought Ann, one of the unsuspecting volunteers, back into the room. We told her to go to the board and draw a picture following directions from Carol. She was not allowed to ask any questions. Carol had to describe how to draw the picture without saying, "Draw Woody Woodpecker's head," and she was not allowed to view Ann's picture. Carol's back was to Ann, and neither could look at the other.

Carol's description is on p. 41. You may wish to draw the picture right below in your text from her directions, not from the picture in figure 2–9.

"Draw a shape like an egg. Below the egg shape draw two vertical, two-inch parallel lines about two inches apart. From the lower right-hand part of the egg shape almost to its center, draw curved lines in the shape of an isosceles triangle, using the lower right-hand side of the egg as one of the base lines of the triangle and take it out to the right. Go to the upper left of where the triangle is but inside the egg shape make a segment about a quarter inch and draw a curved line so that the curve is going in toward the triangle but the bottom line of it will not exceed where the triangle is. Now fill that area in solidly.

Make a wavy line. You are going to divide the egg in half with the height of the wave at the left-hand side of the egg and the trough of it will not extend into the line of the triangle. Now on that solid area that you colored in draw a curved line about a quarter of an inch as an outline around it. Now another wavy line about a half inch from the parallel lines—but in the lower quarter of the divided egg, draw an itsy-bitsy wavy line.

Go to the top of the outline of the solid area that you colored in. Go up about an inch and make a curved line going to the right for about a quarter of an inch. Go straight up about an eighth of an inch from that line and make a sweeping curve coming down about an inch and then big swoop going up and around the top of the egg and attach it to the egg."

You may want to compare your picture with the picture in figure 2–10. This is Ann's perception of Carol's description. Do the pictures look at all alike? From some of Carol's descriptions, you can see that you selectively perceive and structure stimuli according to your experiences. Remember that Carol had to recall mentally

Figure 2-9   Figure 2-10

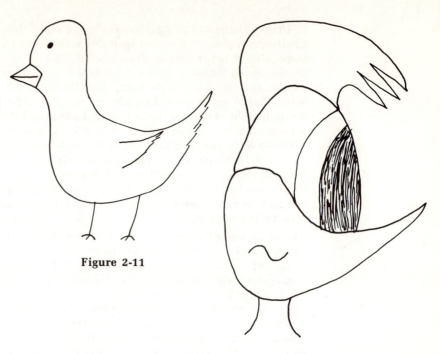

Figure 2-11

Figure 2-12

what she had drawn and describe the drawing to Ann in relatively abstract terms. You would not have given some of Carol's descriptions or some of Ann's responses.

We brought Howie in from the hall, handed him a piece of chalk, and told him to draw whatever Carol said without questioning her or anyone else. As in the first situation, Carol and Howie couldn't see each other. This time, she could tell Howie what to draw but not how to draw it.

Carol simply said, "Draw a woodpecker." Howie's perception of Carol's message is in figure 2–11. She didn't tell him to draw the cartoon character, so he drew what was foremost in his perceptual storehouse of the species woodpecker. Of course, his perception was hampered because he couldn't draw a woodpecker.

Then we called a fourth student, Chuck, into the room. Carol and Chuck worked *together* at the blackboard until their pictures looked very much alike. We have not included their discussion because it is quite long. Chuck's picture is included in figure 2–12.

Compare all four processes and see how they relate to selective perception and communication in general. Now figures 2–9 and 2–12 look similar; however, communication breakdowns may occur. You might find it difficult to get the fourth person to cooperate, for students chosen may think they know better. You will find these personality types in everyday communication situations.

The next series of pictures, figures 2–13 to 2–16, illustrates the problem of cooperation. First the student drew a picture showing how he perceived the instructor, figure 2–13. He then explained it abstractly, figure 2–14. Next, he was told to draw a picture of the instructor, figure 2–15. Figure 2–16 shows that even though two individuals worked closely together for a half-hour, there was no way they could get the pictures in figures 2–13 and 2–16 to look alike. The members of the class enjoyed seeing how others perceive and interpret what they hear.

Figure 2-13

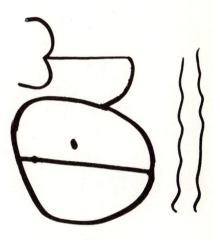

Figure 2-14

Figure 2-15

Figure 2-16

Exercise 15

Perception Implies Meaning

Draw a picture below from the following description found in the *American Heritage Dictionary*. "A large, chiefly aquatic African mammal having dark, thick, almost hairless skin, short legs, and a broad, wide-mouthed muzzle."

What have you drawn? Compare pictures with other class members. Explain why the pictures may be different. If they are not, how did everyone manage to draw the same kind of picture?

As a way to evaluate yourself, complete Journal Exercise 3 on perceptual evaluation at the back of the book.

SUMMARY

Past knowledge and experiences shape your perceptions. You assign meaning to your perceptions and expect others to perceive things in the same way. But the five physical senses are deceptive; they distort reality. You can learn new methods of extending the range of your senses—for example, by smelling a color or hearing your favorite taste. In addition, you have been taught to perceive most of what you have learned: you structure and categorize according to learned systems. You should begin to look at problems from new viewpoints, question old approaches to past perceptions, and seek out new approaches and modifications to existing approaches.

Perception is vitally important to intrapersonal communication. It forces you to examine your perceptual structures and see whether they affect your communication with yourself and others.

Supplementary Reading

It is important to be more sensitive and aware of how you can extend your perceptions. Since the five senses claim a significant control in experiencing life, examine the development of the senses discussed in the following selection by Yi-Fu Tuan. It should help you develop ways to alter your perception by becoming more aware of yourself and others.

COMMON TRAITS IN PERCEPTION: THE SENSES

Yi-Fu Tuan

The earth's surface is highly varied. Even a causal acquaintance with its physical geography and teeming life forms tells us as much. But the ways in which people perceive and evaluate that surface are far more varied. No two persons see the same reality. No two social groups make precisely the same evaluation of the environment. The scientific view itself is culture-bound—one possible perspective among many. As we proceed in this study, the bewildering wealth of viewpoints on both individual and group levels becomes increasingly evident; and we risk losing sight of the fact that however diverse our perceptions of environment, as members of the same species we are constrained to see things a certain way. All human beings share common perceptions, a common world, by virtue of possessing similar organs. The uniqueness of the human perspective should be evident when we pause to ask how the human reality must differ from that of other animals. Contrary to appearances, a person cannot enter imaginatively into the life of his dog: canine sense organs diverge too far from our own for us to leap into the dog's world of smells, sounds, and sights. But with good will one person can enter into the world of another despite differences in age, temperament, and culture. . . . I shall note how human senses differ in range and acuity from those of some other animals, and thus delineate the uniqueness of the human world insofar as this derives from man's perceptual equipment.

Vision The human being has more ways to respond to the world than the five senses of seeing, hearing, smelling, tasting, and touching known to us since the time of Aristotle. For instance, some people are remarkably sensitive to subtle changes in humidity and atmospheric pressure; others appear to be endowed with an unusually acute sense of direction, although the innateness of this faculty has been

Yi-Fu Tuan, *Topophila: A Study of Environmental Perception, Attitudes, and Values,* © 1974, pp. 5–12. Reprinted by permission of Prentice Hall, Inc., Englewood Cliffs, New Jersey.

questioned. Of the traditional five senses man is more consciously dependent on sight to make his way in the world than on the other senses. He is predominantly a visual animal. A larger world is open to him, and far more information that is detailed and specific spatially reaches him through the eyes than through the sensory systems of hearing, smell, taste, and touch. Most people probably regard sight as their most valued faculty, and would rather lose a limb or become deaf or dumb than to sacrifice vision.

Human vision, like that of other primates, has evolved in an arboreal environment. In the dense complex world of a tropical forest, it is more important to see well than to develop an acute sense of smell. In the long course of evolution members of the primate line have acquired large eyes while the snout has shrunk to give the eyes an unimpeded view. Of mammals, only man and some primates enjoy color vision. The red flag is black to the bull. Horses live in a monochrome world. Light visible to human eyes, however, occupies only a very narrow band in the whole electro-magnetic spectrum. Ultraviolet rays are invisible to man, though ants and the honey bees are sensitive to them. Man has no direct perception of infrared rays, unlike the rattlesnake which has receptors tuned in to wavelengths longer than 0.7 microns. The world would look eerily different if human eyes were sensitive to infrared radiation. Then, instead of the darkness of night, we would be able to move easily in a shadowless world where objects glowed with varying degrees of intensity. Human eyes are in fact remarkably discerning in color gradations. The chromatic sensibility of normal human vision boasts a degree of accuracy that is rarely surpassed in spectrophotometry.[2]

Man possesses stereoscopic vision. Human eyes are located at the front, a position that limits the visual field. Unlike, for example, the rabbit a human cannot see what lies behind his head, but the gain in having frontal eyes is that they give a double assurance of information: binocular vision helps man to see things sharply as three-dimensional bodies. This is an innate ability to the extent that an infant soon learns to take cues such as linear perspective and parallax to perceive the round form of the human face. Eight-week-old infants are more capable of discriminating depth and orientation, taking into account size and shape constancy, and are better at performing completion than an empiricist would have predicted.[3] Time and experience, however, are required for the full development of three-dimensional vision. We are so used to seeing things in the round and the world in depth that it is surprising to know that many tricks have to be learnt. People who have been blind from birth as a result of congenital cataract and then have their sights conferred in later life by operation are barely able to recognize objects, far less to see them three-dimensionally. They have to learn the significance of the distribution of light and shadow in the recognition of solids, curves, and relief.

Hands and the Tactile Sense Primates are better able to pick out static details than other mammals. Their food in the forest is largely static so that it is more important for them to perceive objects like fruits, seeds, and shoots by their shape, color, and texture than by minute movements. Like humans, apes and monkeys probably see the environment as a collection of things rather than merely as a pattern. In acquiring this ability, the

[2] Committee on Colorimetry, *The Science of Color* (Washington, D.C.: Optical Society of America, 1966), p. 219.
[3] T. G. R. Bower, "The Visual World of Infants," *Scientific American*, 215, No. 6 (1966), 90.

development of hands, strong and dexterous, is almost as important as the evolution of three-dimensional vision. Monkeys, apes, and man are probably the only animals that can fiddle with things, pick them up, and examine them from all sides. Paws are far less effective than hands, and among primate hands those of the human being combine strength with unmatched precision.[4]

Touch, the haptic sense, in fact provides human beings with a vast amount of information concerning the world. It takes no special skill for a person to feel the difference between a smooth pane of glass and one etched in grooves 1/2,500 of an inch deep. Blindfolded and with ears plugged to remove auditory cues, a man can nevertheless tell the difference between plastic, metal, paper, or wood by gently tapping the surface with a fingernail. Practice improves the sensitivity. The professional cloth feeler in textile houses can judge subtle differences in the quality of fabrics with amazing accuracy. It is not even necessary for him to use his fingers; passing a stick over the cloth will do.[5]

The fundamental nature of the sense of touch is brought home to us when we reflect that, without sight a person can still operate with a high degree of efficiency in the world, but without the tactual sense it is doubtful that he can survive. We are always "in touch." For instance, at this moment we may be feeling the pressure of the chair against our posterior and the pressure of the pencil in our hand. Touch is the direct experience of resistance, the direct experience of the world as a system of resistances and pressures that persuade us of the existence of a reality independent of our imaginings. To see is not yet to believe: hence Christ offered himself to be *touched* by the doubting apostle. The importance of touch to knowledge is suggested by the English idiom "to keep in touch" or "to be out of touch," used not only with regard to persons but to fields of learning.

Hearing   Auditory sensitivity in man is not especially acute. Hearing is less essential to primates, including humans, than to carnivores who track their prey. Compared with the ears of tracking killers those of primates are small and they lack twisting mobility. The average young human's hearing has a range extending roughly from 16 to 20,000 cycles per second. If a person is sensitive to a pitch lower than 16 cycles, he may suffer the annoyance of being able to hear his own heartbeat. The upper limit of the human hearing range is modest compared with that of cats and bats: these mammals respond to sound of up to 50,000 and 120,000 cycles per second respectively. The human ear appears to be most sensitive to sound at a pitch corresponding to a child's or woman's cry. It is adapted specifically to the survival of the species and generally to engaging the world through auditory cues.

The eyes gain far more precise and detailed information about the environment than the ears but we are usually more touched by what we hear than by what we see. The sound of rain pelting against leaves, the roll of thunder, the whistling of wind in tall grass, and the anguished cry excite us to a degree that visual imagery can seldom match. Music is for most people a stronger emotional experience than looking at pictures or scenery. Why is this? Partly, perhaps, because we cannot close our ears

[4] Bernard Campbell, *Human Evolution: An Introduction to Man's Adaptations* (Chicago: Aldine-Atherton, 1966), pp. 161–62.
[5] Lorus J. Milne and Margery Milne, *The Senses of Animals and Men* (New York: Atheneum, 1962), pp. 18–20; Owen Lowenstein, *The Senses* (Baltimore: Penguin, 1966).

as we can our eyes. We feel more vulnerable to sound.[6] "Hearing" has the connotation of passivity (receptivity) that "seeing" does not have. Another reason may be that one of the most important sensations of the human infant, and perhaps even of the foetus, is the beat of the mother's heart. Desmond Morris, for example, thinks that this explains the fact that a mother (even when she is left-handed) normally holds the infant in such a way that his head rests against the left breast.[7] It also seems true that a human infant is sensitive to sound, making distinctions between the pleasant, the soothing, and the disturbing, long before it can discriminate with any subtlety visually.

The importance of hearing to the human grasp of reality is emphasized by the acute sense of loss for those who have suddenly become deaf. Contrary to expectations, the psychological effects of sudden deafness can be as debilitating as the sudden loss of sight. Deep depression, loneliness, and paranoid tendencies are some of the consequences. With deafness, life seems frozen and time lacks progression. Space itself contracts, for our experience of space is greatly extended by the auditory sense which provides information of the world beyond the visual field. At first, a world that seems to have lost its dynamism appears less demanding and nervous; it induces a feeling of detachment and peace, as happens in a pleasant way when the sounds of the city are muffled by light rain or a blanket of snow. But soon the silence, the severe loss of information, induces anxiety, dissociation, and withdrawal in the deaf.[8]

Smell A man cannot project himself into a dog's world if for no other reason than the chasm in the olfactory sensitivity of the two species. The dog's sense of smell is at least a hundred times more acute than that of man. Though carnivores and some ungulates have sharp vision, they place greater reliance on their olfactory receptors to survive in their world, in comparison with the primates. Of course the sense of smell is also important to primates. It plays a large part in the fundamental processes of feeding and mating. Modern man, however, tends to neglect the olfactory sense. His ideal environment would seem to require the exclusion of "smells" of any kind. The word "odor" itself nearly always connotes bad odor. This trend is regrettable, for the human nose is in fact an amazingly proficient organ for sniffing out information. With practice a person can classify the world into such odoriferous categories as alliaceous, ambrosiac, pepperminty, aromatic, ethereal, foul, fragrant, goaty, or nauseous.

Odor has the power to evoke vivid, emotionally-charged memories of past events and scenes. A whiff of sage may call to mind an entire complex of sensations: the image of great rolling plains covered with grass and specked by clumps of sagebrush, the brightness of the sun, the heat, the bumpiness of the road. Whence this power? Several factors come into play. For one, the power of an odor to cast us into the past may be related to the fact that the cortex with its vast memory store evolved from the part of the brain originally concerned with smell. For another, as children, not only were our noses more sensitive but they were closer to the earth, to

[6] G. M. Wyburn, R. W. Pickford, and R. J. Hirst, *Human Senses and Perception* (Edinburgh: Oliver and Boyd, 1964), pp. 66.
[7] Desmond Morris, *The Naked Ape* (London: Transworld Publishers, Corgi edition, 1968), pp. 95–96.
[8] P. H. Knapp, "Emotional Aspects of Hearing Loss," *Psychomatic Medicine*, 10 (July/August 1948), 203–22.

flower beds, tall grass, and the damp soil that give off odors. In adulthood, a chance encounter with the fragrance of a haystack may jolt our memory back nostalgically to the past. A further point is that seeing is selective and reflects experience. When we return to the scene of our childhood, not only the landscape has changed but the way we see it. We cannot recapture fully the essential feel of a visual world belonging to our past without the help of a sensory experience that has not changed, for instance, the strong odor of decaying seaweed.

Perceiving with
All the Senses

Responding to the world through sight differs from responding to it through the other senses in several important respects. For instance, seeing is "objective;" seeing—as the expression goes—is believing, but we tend to distrust information obtained through the ears; it is "hearsay" or "rumor." Seeing does not involve our emotions deeply. We can see through the window of an air-conditioned bus that the slum is ugly and undesirable, but how undesirable reaches us with pungent force only when we open the window and catch a whiff from the malodorous sewers. The person who just "sees" is an onlooker, a sightseer, someone not otherwise involved with the scene. The world perceived through the eyes is more abstract than that known to us through the other senses. The eyes explore the visual field and abstract from it certain objects, points of focus, perspectives. But the taste of lemon, the texture of warm skin, and the sound of rustling leaves reach us as just these sensations. The visual field is far larger than the fields of the other senses. Distant objects can only be *seen;* hence, we have the tendency to regard *seen* objects as "distant"—as not calling forth any strong emotional response—even though they may in point of fact be close to us.

A human being perceives the world through all his senses simultaneously. The information potentially available to him is immense. In man's daily projects, however, only a small portion of his innate power to experience is called into use. What sense organ is given special exercise varies with the individual and his culture. In modern society man comes to rely more and more on sight. Space for him is bounded and static, a frame or matrix for objects. Without objects and boundaries space is empty. It is empty because there is nothing to see even though it might be filled with wind. Compare this attitude with that of the Aivilik Eskimo on Southampton Island. To the Eskimo, space is not pictorial or boxed in, but something always in flux, creating its own dimensions moment by moment. He learns to orient himself with all senses alert. He has to during certain times in winter when sky and earth merge and appear to be made of the same substance. There is then "no middle distance, no perspective, no outline, nothing that the eye can cling to except thousands of smokey plumes of snow running along the ground before the wind—a land without bottom or edge."[9] Under such conditions the Eskimo cannot rely on the points of reference given by permanent landmarks: he must depend on the shifting relationships of snow contours, on the types of snow, wind, salt air, and ice crack. The direction and smell of the wind is a guide, together with the feel of ice and snow under his feet. The invisible wind plays a large role in the life of the Aivilik Eskimo. His language includes at least twelve unrelated terms for various winds. He learns to orient himself by them. On horizonless days he lives in an acoustic-olfactory space.

[9] Edmund Carpenter, Frederick Varley, and Robert Flaherty, *Eskimo* (Toronto: University of Toronto Press, 1959), pages unnumbered.

The medieval cathedral fascinates the modern tourist for various reasons, but one that has received little comment is this: the cathedral offers him an environment that stimulates the simultaneous use of three or four sense receptors. It has sometimes been said that the steel-and-glass skyscraper is the modern equivalent of the medieval cathedral. Actually, apart from the vertical bias the two buildings have very little in common. They do not illustrate the same principles of construction, they are not put to the same use, and their symbolic meanings are entirely different. Again, apart from verticality, the sensual and aesthetic experiences provided by these two structures are antipodal. The modern skyscraper caters largely to sight, though the varying types of floor covering provide changes in tactile stimuli. If there is sound, it is probably "musak" which is meant to be audible but not heard. By contrast, the experience of the interior of a cathedral involves sight, sound, touch, and smell.[10] Each sense reinforces the other so that together they clarify the structure and substance of the entire building, revealing its essential character.

Perception and Activity

Perception is an activity, a reaching out to the world. Sense organs are minimally operative when they are not actively used. Our tactile sense is very delicate but to tell differences in the texture or hardness of surfaces it is not sufficient to put a finger on them; the finger has to move over them. It is possible to have eyes and not see, ears and not hear.

The playfulness of the mammalian young and, in particular, the human child, has often been observed. For the very young the playing is not directed by sustained purposes. A ball is thrown, blocks are piled up and knocked down largely as manifestations of animal spirit. In this aimless playing the infant learns about the world. He develops body coordination. By moving about, touching, and manipulating he learns the reality of objects and the structuring of space. However, unlike other primates, at an early stage in the human child's growth (three or four years), his playing begins to be governed by themes. It occurs in the context of stories he tells himself. These are transfigured versions of his experiences in a world ruled by adults, of tales told by them, and bits of conversation overheard. His activities and explorations, then, are increasingly directed by cultural values. Although all human beings have similar sense organs, how their capacities are used and developed begin to diverge at an early age. As a result, not only do attitudes to environment differ but the actualized capacity of the senses differs, so that people in one culture may acquire sharp noses for scent while those in another acquire deep stereoscopic vision. Both worlds are predominantly visual: one will be enriched by fragrances, the other by the acute three-dimensionality of objects and spaces.

ADDITIONAL READING

Allport, F. *Theories of Perception.* New York: John Wiley & Sons, 1955.
  A review and examination of the trends in psychological thinking about perception. It offers solutions to some perceptual problems, and it goes beyond analysis to discuss existing theories and summarize the processes underlying perception.

Bartley, S. Howard. *Principles of Perception.* New York: Harper & Row, 1969.
  A behaviorally oriented text on human perception that is highly technical and heavily psychological and physiological in emphasis. It portrays the human organism's immediate reactions to the environment.

Beardslee, David C., and Wertheimer, Michael. *Readings in Perception.* Princeton, N.J.: D. Van Nostrand, 1958.

[10] Richard Neutra, *Survival Through Design* (New York: Oxford University Press, 1969), pp. 139–40.

A collection of readings on perception that dwells on sensory psychology. Although not an up-to-date book, it contains articles that help establish definitions and criteria for understanding sense distortion. Studies reflect the core of the experimental psychology of perception, which views events in terms of personality and motivation.

Dember, William N. *Psychology of Perception.* New York: Holt, Rinehart & Winston, 1960.
A discussion of the psychological rationale behind psychophysics, with an elaboration of tests of threshold levels of stimulation. Treatments of the development of visual perception and the influence on perception of the sensory, cognitive, and motivational context make helpful background reading.

Fabun, Don. *Communications: The Transfer of Meaning.* Beverly Hills, Calif.: Glencoe Press, 1968.
An easy-to-understand description of communication. Examples and diagrams reveal the difficulties of human communication.

Frank, Joseph. *You.* New York: Harcourt Brace Jovanovich, 1972.
A text that encourages self-examination. The first part of the book deals with the senses, the second part with how you perceive yourself and your relationship with your world.

Ralston, Melvin, and Cox, Don Richard. *Emblems of Reality.* New York: Glencoe Press, 1973.
A book interspersed with cartoons, photographs, and quotations supplementing discussions, commentaries, and writing assignments that center on self-introspection. The purpose of the text is to raise questions about how you perceive the patterns in your life experience.

"Yes," I answered you last night;
"No," this morning, sir, I say:
Colors seen by candle-light
Will not look the same by day.
—Elizabeth Barrett Browning

Like all weak men he laid an exaggerated stress on not chang-
ing one's mind.
—W. Somerset Maugham

3. IDENTITY ADJUSTMENT

OBJECTIVES   In this chapter we ask you to do the following:

1. Recognize the human need to maintain psychological balance between personal attitudes, values, and beliefs and the new information constantly bombarding the senses.

2. Identify your own needs that operate at each level of Abraham Maslow's hierarchy of human motivation.

3. Determine the extent to which your needs, goals, and expectations direct your intrapersonal communication and actions.

4. Analyze situations in which you experience conflict in attempting to satisfy your needs and experience imbalance or dissonance among your cognitions.

5. Investigate the tactics you use to rationalize dissonant information, thereby restoring your mental balance.

6. Defend one of your strongly held beliefs in the face of challenge from your peers.

For each of us, our perceptions are our realities. We decide what is truth, wisdom, or beauty from the experiences we associate with these abstract terms. These value judgments are not a part of the objects and events; they are evaluations that we make internally. Thus they differ from person to person, just as our range of life experiences differs. However, no matter how much our perceptions may differ from those of others, we continually define our self-images and our world orientations as if our perceptions were accurate. Yet we meet pressures to change our identities (self-images) as we accept or adjust to new ideas and experiences.

To maintain a consistent view of ourselves and our external reality, we selectively perceive and expose ourselves to people and events around us, so that future observations conform to what we *need, want,* and *expect* to find outside ourselves. However, we cannot completely control all information coming to us. Often information, individuals, and even our own actions conflict with our beliefs. When this happens, we experience strong pressures to reduce or eliminate the conflict. Sometimes we are able to ignore the information or its source. Generally, we rationalize or distort the information so that it will conform with our orientation. But on other occasions we may have to reassess our attitudes, alter our world views, and even adjust our self-concepts.

Now that you have worked through chapters 1 and 2, you should be able to identify your self-image and recognize the assumptions and perceptual frame of reference through which you process new events and experiences. The information and exercises in this chapter will allow you to investigate further the influences on your intrapersonal communication behavior—the universal human needs that direct your perceptions and actions, and the rationalizing tactics that help you to maintain a consistent internal reality or to adjust to new views.

ATTITUDES & BELIEFS   NEW INFORMATION

SEEING WHAT WE NEED

Underlying our decisions as to what is good or bad, useful or useless, or right or wrong are the human needs that we all must satisfy to maintain life. Persons or objects become valuable if they help us to meet these needs and harmful if they block this need satisfaction. Abraham Maslow provides one frequently cited classification of human needs and an explanation of our motivation to act to fulfill our needs. Maslow identifies five levels of needs common to everyone, viewing the operation of our needs as a hierarchy with some needs more critical for survival than others.

His five levels of needs follow, with the lowest being most critical for survival:

1. *Physiological needs:* The human hungers for food, water, sleep, sex, and other activity.

2. *Security needs:* The human needs for physical and material protection and safety, for shelter, and for an organized, predictable life pattern.

3. *Belongingness and love needs:* The human needs to belong with others—to give and receive love and affection.

4. *Esteem needs:* The human needs to hold a high self-evaluation— derived from both self-respect and the esteem of others.

5. *Self-actualization needs:* The human needs to achieve what each person knows can be accomplished.[1]

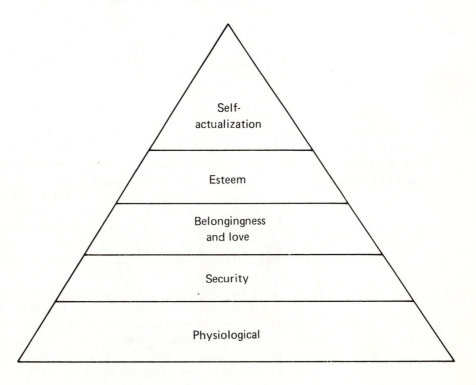

[1] Abraham H. Maslow, *Motivation and Personality* (New York: Harper & Row, 1954), pp. 80–92.

The principle that the lowest need level must be satisfied before a higher order of need can be approached is essential to an understanding of Maslow's hierarchical representation. The lowest need level dominates behavior until it is satisfied. Then the next lowest level emerges, dominates, and directs behavior. For example, the physiological needs for food and water (level 1) must be met before one can seek to secure a claim to food and water (level 2) or join in group activity (level 3).

Maslow's description of the general areas of human needs does not imply a static condition. The needs that we try to satisfy change as important events influence our lives. If John is actively seeking a measure of esteem (level 4) by campaigning for the presidency of his service club, he will probably redirect his efforts when he learns that a reorganization of his company is about to eliminate his job as bookkeeper, his security (level 2). Likewise, several levels of needs may be simultaneously operating on an individual, and one set of actions may partially satisfy them all. For example, the individual gaining employment in a profession acquires the economic resources to provide for physiological hungers (level 1), satisfies some security needs (level 2) with the regular life pattern that the job imposes, and possibly gains recognition or esteem (level 4) from the status of the position.

The five need areas generally apply to all of us, but we do not all operate on the same level at the same time. Further, the means through which we individually satisfy needs on a given level differ according to the values, attitudes, and beliefs we have learned through past associations. And a strong determining factor of what we choose to perceive in a given situation, or even of the situations to which we subject ourselves, will be the needs we are attempting to satisfy. Our own behavior becomes more understandable when we can identify our dominating needs.

MAKING WHAT WE WANT OF OURSELVES

In acting to satisfy your needs and goals, you have no doubt found that your needs frequently collide. Two needs often conflict, so that action satisfying one need requires that the other need remain unmet. For example, your desire to remain cool during the summer conflicts with your desire to conserve the energy required to run an air conditioner. One need will win out; the other need will remain, or at best be compromised. In this case, you might decide to run the air conditioner only when the temperature climbs above 90°F. Regardless of your decision, some tension or discomfort will remain because you have been forced to violate at least one of your private beliefs.

Whenever you recognize an inconsistency or incompatibility among your opinions and values, or between your beliefs and the information or values of others, you experience a psychological tension called *cognitive dissonance*. The term *cognition* refers to "any knowledge, opinion, or belief about the environment, about oneself, or about one's behavior."[2] Dissonance exists when you are aware that your separate cognitions conflict or

[2] Leon Festinger, *A Theory of Cognitive Dissonance* (Evanston, Ill.: Row-Peterson, 1957), p. 3.

Exercise 16

Personal Need Analysis

As an individual exercise, use the five need levels of Maslow's hierarchy to list the specific needs operating in your life situation at each level.

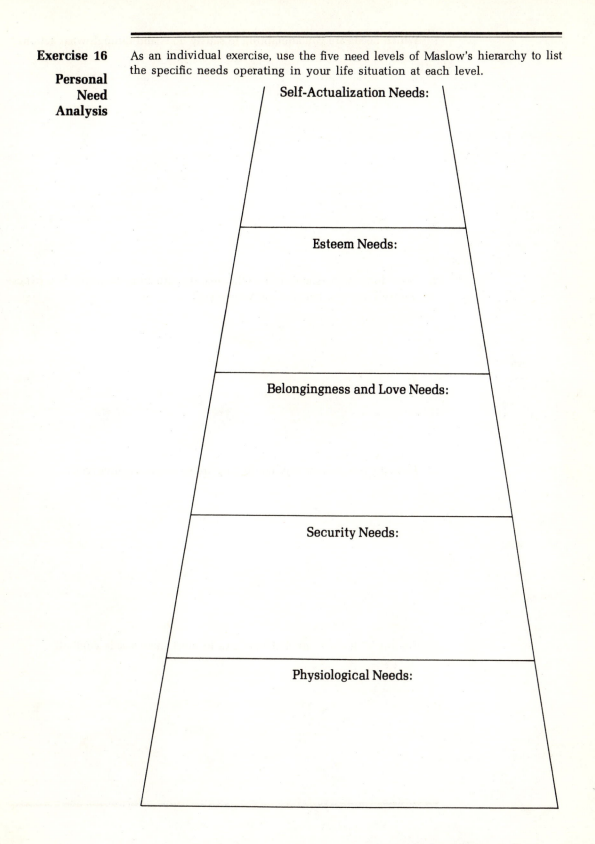

Self-Actualization Needs:

Esteem Needs:

Belongingness and Love Needs:

Security Needs:

Physiological Needs:

1. Which needs are you attempting to satisfy now, and through what actions?

2. How do these personal needs influence the situations to which you expose yourself and the perceptions you select?

3. How do you process any conflicting information reaching you?

4. Do any of the actions that you take to meet these needs conflict?

that they do not correspond to new information that you have acquired. The opposite condition, the psychologically desirable situation, is termed *consonance*.

Cognitive dissonance operates as a motivating force requiring you to take action to reduce the psychological tension. Making any decision will reduce the tension that required you to act, but further actions are often necessary to justify your decision. You will attempt to rationalize all information about the decision to convince yourself that the choice you made was the "best" possible. The following examples illustrate the operation of cognitive dissonance and the variety of actions necessary to reduce the psychological tension. Reducing conflict allows you to maintain mental balance and stability.

Conflict between alternative actions exists not only when you choose which need to satisfy, but also when you choose which option to take in satisfying one need. Consider the number of attractive options open as you choose a career area. You might construct an image of yourself holding an important position in business, a partnership in a law firm, or an appointment on a university faculty. At the same time, you may want to marry the man or woman you love now and start to raise a family. The range of choices that you find acceptable constitutes your *latitude of acceptance*. Conversely, the range of options that you consider unacceptable constitutes your *latitude of rejection*. You can usually follow only one option. And from the time that you make your decision, you begin an active campaign to assure yourself that the decision is right. Remember that it's necessary to do this for mental stability!

Assume that you chose to marry at a young age and raise a family. You married your high school sweetheart, took a factory job, and now have a young child. As your friends begin to finish their studies in prelaw, premedicine, journalism, or business, your career aspirations begin to resurface. You feel that your marriage has "prevented" you from achieving a better employment position, but you have invested six years in your marriage and job. You need to convince yourself that your choice was correct: your happiness and continuing satisfaction depend on it. So, as you look at your graduating friends, you choose to see your friend with teaching credentials who is stuck driving a cab or typing, or your friend with the master's degree in business administration who is "managing" produce or the cash register in the local supermarket. You "know" that you are better off, and you can continue to live happily with your life choice.

Consider the same situation from the perspective of someone who chose to forgo marriage and family to obtain an advance degree. Leaving the graduation ceremony with your diploma in hand, you visit the home of high-school friends who married in their teens. Their home is far nicer than the trailer you have been renting; their car is six years newer than yours; and their children are cute and fun to play with. You cannot avoid comparing your situation with theirs, but how do you rationalize your choice when you have few material objects to show for the past six years' work? You might smile, knowing that it will be twenty years before the mortgage on the lovely home is paid off, or you might feel some degree of superiority because you don't "need" material objects as a measure of your self-worth. Finally, you might choose to believe that their happiness is an illusion; after all, kids tie you down, and even the "best" modern marriages do not seem to last.

Obviously, each decision you make to satisfy your needs precludes a number of other life options. The ability to make your decisions seem right, good, and the best possible—while making the other alternatives appear wrong, bad, or undesirable—is essential to your sanity and happiness.

Exercise 17

Life Goals and Options

As an individual exercise, identify the current range of possibilities for your life goals.

Educational goals	Marriage and family goals	Career goals	Material object goals

1. Which of your identified goals are most important?

2. Are you actively pursuing these goals? If not, why?

3. Do any of your goals conflict? Explain.

4. Why do you consider these goals to be important?

5. How do you react when a friend achieves one of your unmet goals?

A number of theories have been developed to explain how we make our choices continue to seem right. These theories, generally labeled *consistency* or *balance theories*, all assume that:

1. People need consistency among their values, beliefs, and attitudes to maintain psychological health.

2. People will selectively perceive and expose themselves to those messages supporting their decisions and will attempt to rationalize any information indicating that their choices are undesirable.

Leon Festinger's theory of cognitive dissonance is the most applicable analysis for understanding our communication within ourselves. Festinger reasons that when our decisions meet certain needs, but also prevent satisfaction of other needs, the mental tensions thus produced motivate us to act to reduce the dissonant state.

> ... I am proposing that dissonance, that is, the existence of nonfitting relations among cognitions, is a motivating factor in its own right. By the term *cognition*, I mean any knowledge, opinion, or belief about the environment, about oneself, or about one's behavior. Cognitive dissonance can be seen as an antecedent condition which leads to activity oriented toward dissonance reduction just as hunger leads to an activity oriented toward hunger reduction.[3]

Festinger goes on to detail four types of situations in which people experience dissonance.

The first type of situation, in which *you have made a choice between two or more alternative courses of action*, has already been described. Depending on the importance of the rejected alternative, the dissonance and the felt need to reduce the dissonance will be either great or small. The decision to buy a foreign economy car instead of an American compact car leaves you with one car and not the other. Because this choice has probably left you with payments to make over an extended period of time, you will long be reminded of the option you chose. You will probably seek information that reinforces your choice of the foreign car as correct and identifies the choice of the rejected American compact car as wrong (this action is called *selective perception*). You will read claims of high engine performance and low pollution emissions in European cars, talk to friends who make amazing mileage claims, and recognize the maneuverability of your car in heavy traffic. You will try to avoid those people who claim that American mechanics cannot service foreign cars and that foreign car parts are expensive and difficult to obtain.

If you selectively expose yourself to certain information situations that promise to reinforce your beliefs, and if you selectively perceive the available information to make it conform to your needs, wants, and expectations, why can you still experience cognitive dissonance? What do you do with the information that disagrees with your personal life views? Three other types of dissonance-producing situations that Festinger explored

[3] Ibid.

illustrate attempts to restore balance in the face of conflicting beliefs and information.

A second type of dissonance-producing situation occurs when *you are asked to say or do something that differs from your private opinion.* Consider Mr. Hill, a teacher who judges his classroom to be a success. His students participate in class discussions, put in extra effort to produce interesting group projects, and relate ideas presented in class to their daily life experiences. Because of a new school policy, he must individualize his course, computerize the evaluation process, and substitute written unit directions and resource materials for instructor presentations and class discussions. He must exchange the method of instruction that he practices and believes is effective for an untried approach. As he teaches with the new format, he is likely to seek ways to reduce dissonance by looking for classroom successes that he can attribute to the new method—students who learn more when they are allowed to work at their own rate, students' enthusiasm for independent study, and so on. Or he may minimize his belief in classroom methodology as the key to success. Perhaps he will ultimately change his belief and accept the new instructional approach as the most successful classroom procedure. Regardless of the tactic he uses, to continue in his chosen profession of teaching, he must convince himself that he is using the best methods available.

A third situation causing dissonance is one in which *you are exposed to information that contradicts your beliefs.* For example, you have always believed that any organization resembling a fraternity or sorority is bad because it has exclusive membership restrictions. Then you discover that all of the fund-raising projects of a local sorority support a school for handicapped children in your community. To reduce the mental conflict caused when new information challenges your personal belief, you will probably find a way to retain some of your opposition to fraternities and sororities (most of them do have restrictive membership provisions) while acknowledging that good works often result from their activities. In this situation, you separate and *compartmentalize* the original belief and the conflicting new information: this compartmentalization allows you to accommodate both.

The fourth dissonance-producing situation that Festinger identified arises when *someone disagrees with you.* The amount of dissonance you experience varies, depending on the importance of your relationship with the other person and the significance of the disagreement. If the person is a close friend, you might decide that the information he has is incorrect; you will discredit the message. If you have no feeling for the other person, it may be easy to discredit the person as a source of information. If the issue is of relative importance and the other person is neither a close friend nor a casual acquaintance, you may change the message, deciding "what was really meant." Your other option is to ignore both the person and the message.

RATIONALIZING TACTICS   Behavior to restore balance in dissonant situations involves some form of *rationalization.* When you cannot, through selective perception, avoid encounters with information or individuals opposing your beliefs, you mentally attempt to change some factor of the situation to make it tolerable and thereby, to restore balance. In summary, actions to restore balance include these tactics:

1. Ignoring the information and the source;

2. Discrediting the source of discrepant information;

3. Discrediting the dissonance-producing message;

4. Compartmentalizing the private belief and the discrepant information so that you can tolerate both;

5. Changing the original intention of the message;

6. Changing your attitude or belief in the direction of the new information;

7. Deciding that worse perils—i.e., more dangerous alternatives—exist.

When you have no way of judging the validity of dissonant information, you may reduce your psychological tension by denying the competence of its source. For example, what credentials does your neighbor, the plumber, have to recommend treatment of athlete's foot? On the other hand, if the source of information is a close friend or member of your family, it may be easier to reject the information—at least until it can be further verified— than to question the individual's intention or competence. For example, you decide that your sister's claim, that all nurses will be required to complete a bachelor's degree within five years to keep their licenses, should not cause you immediate worry about your nursing credentials. You may even be able to hold two conflicting judgments if you are able to keep them mentally separate. You may be able to congratulate your neighbor for her victory in the city tennis tournament even though you always disagree about national politics, if you believe that athletic ability and political judgments have no inherent connection.

Occasionally, you may find that the easiest way to rationalize dissonant information is to distort or change the intention of the message. This is the tactic that Ms. Jones, the receptionist, uses; she wants to remain hostile toward her employer for checking to see that she arrives on the job before 9:00 A.M. each morning. She will probably not credit her employer with being concerned that someone answers the company phone at all times during working hours.

A drastic situation, and the new information that it consequently brings, may also cause you to modify an existing belief. When it is your home that the volunteer fire department saves, you will probably contribute to their equipment fund, although you have ignored contribution appeals in prior years. One last rationalizing tactic that may produce behavior at variance with your private belief, without changing that belief, is the realization that a worse peril or more undesirable situation could result. You may disagree with a company policy and yet enforce it because you decide that unemployment will be more personally undesirable than a compromise of your belief.

To discover what dissonance-reducing tactics you use yourself, complete Journal Exercise 4 at the back of the book.

Exercise 18

Situational Rationalizing

In this individual exercise, assume that you are in the market for a motorcycle. You propose several good reasons for buying one: a motorcycle will provide inexpensive transportation and excitement for your leisure hours—and besides, your friends own them. You know generally the size that you want—something larger than a motor scooter (your perception of the Honda 50) but definitely smaller than the largest Harley-Davidson. The decision narrows down to three models: (1) the Honda 90, (2) the Yamaha 125, and (3) the Suzuki II. After some investigation, you purchase the Yamaha 125; it costs more than either the Honda or the Suzuki, but it has more power. For the first few months, you have a marvelous time with your new purchase, and you learn much more about its capabilities and top performance. Then a government committee investigating safety on the roads publishes an extensive research report stating that motorcycle accidents have increased threefold in the past six months, while the purchase of new motorcycles has increased only twofold.

With this background in mind, use Leon Festinger's analysis of cognitive dissonance and the discussion of rationalizing tactics to complete the following instructions:

1. Explain your first few months of activity with your new purchase.

2. Use two of the rationalizing tactics to explain how you would probably behave after reading the government report.

3. In your own words, state Festinger's premise about how people maintain cognitive balance, and use this motorcycle situation to illustrate his premise.

Exercise 19

Challenge to Personal Belief

The objectives of this group exercise, which can be performed as a small group or a large class, are (1) to examine a strongly held personal belief, and (2) to evaluate intrapersonal communication behavior when a group situation challenges a personal belief.

Choose a belief that you hold strongly—strongly enough that you would feel discomfort or hostility if someone were to challenge either the belief or your right to express it. According to the procedure that follows, explain your belief and respond to challenges from either the small group or the entire class.

1. *Position Paper*: In several paragraphs, explain the experiences that have caused you to adopt the belief. What selective perceptions do you make to maintain this belief? Which situations do you expose yourself to (or avoid) in order to hold the belief? Define the latitude of acceptance (the range of similar positions you can tolerate) and the latitude of rejection (the range of positions or alternatives you reject) due to your belief.

2. *Presentation of Your Belief*: In a three-to-five-minute oral presentation, explain your belief and how it is based on your experiences to a group of your classmates. Include the material you discussed in the position paper. (Each member of the group will present a belief.)

3. *Challenge to Belief*: In a one-to-two-minute oral response, challenge the belief a classmate has expressed by (a) denying the person's right to hold the belief, (b) questioning the classmate's interpretation of experiences that support the belief, and/or (c) claiming that similar experiences have led you to adopt an opposite belief. Each group member will challenge the belief that one other member has presented. (You may need to set aside momentarily a private agreement with another group member as you attempt to challenge a belief.)

4. *Defense of Belief*: In a two-to-three-minute rebuttal, re-establish your belief as you originally presented it.

5. *Group Discussion of Belief*: A brief session allowing all group members to challenge and defend beliefs further may follow.

6. *Evaluation*: Answer the following questions based on your experience during the session on challenges to personal belief.

    a. Were you personally challenged? What type of information challenged you?

b. If you were not challenged, why was your belief secure?

c. What type of information is most threatening to your ability to maintain this belief?

d. How did you feel when your peers attempted to shake a belief that is an essential component of your value system?

e. Did your belief change in any way as a result of this experience?

SUMMARY   There is a group of theories that is important to our understanding of intrapersonal communication; these theories attempt to explain the psychological need to maintain balance or consonance between our self-concept (attitudes, values, and beliefs) and the new information constantly bombarding our senses. We carefully avoid or attempt to distort situations that produce conflict, and we continually define our own "truths," or our reality, and seek situations that will confirm our judgment. Consequently, we rationalize our experiences to conform with what we need, want, and expect them to represent.

Abraham Maslow's hierarchical representation of universal human needs provides one explanation of why we choose certain situations in which to operate. We are motivated to fulfill certain kinds of needs. Leon Festinger's analysis of psychological tension and cognitive dissonance, which we experience when events and the environment contradict our beliefs, further explains our actions to make our environment conform to what we want. Using what he calls rationalizing tactics, we attempt to restore and maintain balance in our environment.

SUPPLEMENTARY READING

William Haney, in the selection that follows, explains four conclusions of psychologist Carl Rogers. They concern the behavior of individuals attempting to maintain a consistent self-identity and world orientation while meeting changing needs. Rogers' contribution to the material in this chapter is his notion that a change in identity is positive—personal growth.

FRAME OF REFERENCE

William V. Haney

Frame of reference . . . has been defined as:

A system of standards or values, usually merely implicit, underlying and to some extent controlling an action, or the expression of any attitude, belief, or idea. [4]

Carl Rogers offers several propositions[5] which serve as a rationale for the validity and utility of the frame of reference construct.

1. *Every individual exists in a continually changing world of experience of which he is the center.*

Rogers holds that each of us is at the core of his own world and everything else is happening, developing, occurring about him—(not unlike Ptolemy's homocentric notion of the earth as the center of the universe). It is painfully obvious that man is the most egocentric organism on earth, and surely no one can be more self-centered than the human infant. The baby will outgrow much of this, of course, but hardly all of it. But it would seem that one who is approaching emotional maturity has already recognized that egocentrism is a substantial part of being human. Once one accepts this frailty he is in an excellent state to begin to compensate for it and to grow beyond it. The truly arrogant person, however, is the man or woman who has never made and perhaps cannot make this admission. For so long as one can shield himself from a recognition of his fallibility, he need not expend energy in growing and he need not submit to the unknowns and possible pain of *change.*

2. *The individual reacts to his world as he experiences and perceives it and thus this perceptual world is, for the individual, "reality."*

Reprinted from *Communication and Organizational Behavior* by William V. Haney (Homewood, Ill.: Richard D. Irwin, 1973).

[4] H. B. English and A. C. English, *A Comprehensive Dictionary of Psychological and Psychoanalytical Terms* (New York: Longmans, Green & Co., 1958).
[5] Paraphrased from C. R. Rogers, *Client-Centered Therapy* (Boston: Houghton Mifflin, 1951), pp. 483, 484, 487, 494.

Rogers put quotes around *reality* to indicate that it is not the "real" reality. Consider these definitions of perception: "The point of reality contact, the door to reality appraisal";[6] the "structuring of stimuli"[7] and the "organization of stimuli";[8] and "the way in which the person structures his world and himself."[9] But regardless of how invalid and incomplete it may be, one's personalized reality is the only one he has and therefore the only one to which he responds.

3. *The individual has one basic tendency and striving which is to actualize, maintain, and enhance himself.*

Rogers writes of the *actualizing tendency* as "the inherent tendency of the organism to develop all its capacities in ways to serve to maintain or enhance the organism. It involves not only the tendency to meet . . . 'deficiency needs' for air, food, water, and the like, but also more generalized activities. . . . It is development toward autonomy and away from heteronomy, or control by external forces."[10] He subscribes to Angyal's statement: "Life is an autonomous event which takes place between the organism and the environment. Life processes do not merely tend to preserve life but transcend the momentary status quo of the organism, expanding itself continually and imposing its autonomous determination upon an ever increasing realm of events."[11]

According to Frenkel-Brunswik:

It would appear that we do not always see ourselves as we are but instead perceive the environment in terms of our own need. Self-perception and perception of the environment actually merge in the service of these needs. Thus, the perceptual distortions of ourselves and the environment fulfill an important function in our psychological household.[12]

The role of *needs* and *motivation* in influencing perception and therefore behavior is clearly [an] important [one] . . .

4. *Therefore, the best vantage point for understanding another's behavior is from that person's internal frame of reference.*

This conclusion follows logically from Rogers' preceding propositions but this does not necessarily make it easy to utilize the frame of reference concept. The individual's internal frame of reference *is* his subjective world. "Only he knows it fully. It can never be known to another except through empathic inference and then can never be perfectly known."[13]

Probably the greatest single deterrent to one's accurately visualizing another's frame of reference is his *own*. An analogy will suggest why this is so.

[6] G. S. Klein, "The Personal World through Perception," *Perception: An Approach to Personality,* ed. R. R. Blake and G. V. Ramsey (New York: Ronald Press, 1951), pp. 328–29.
[7] C.M. Solley and G. Murphy, *Development of the Perceptual World* (New York: Basic Books, 1960), p. 26.
[8] F. A. Beach, "Body Chemistry and Perception," Blake and Ramsey, *op. cit.,* p. 56.
[9] U. Bronfenbrenner, "Toward an Integrated Theory of Personality," *ibid.,* p. 207.
[10] C. R. Rogers, "A Theory of Therapy, Personality, and Interpersonal Relationships, as Developed in the Client-Centered Framework," *Psychology: The Study of a Science,* vol. 3, *Formulations of the Social Context,* ed. Sigmund Koch (New York: McGraw-Hill, 1959), p. 196.
[11] A. Angyal, *Foundations for a Science of Personality* (New York: Commonwealth Fund, 1941).
[12] Else Frenkel-Brunswik, "Personality Theory and Perception," chap. 13 in Blake and Ramsey, *op. cit.,* p. 379.
[13] C. R. Rogers. "A Theory of Therapy . . . ," *op. cit.,* p. 210.

Analogy of the Box

Visualize each of us as the sole and constant tenant of a box with a top, a bottom, and four sides. There is just one window in this box—one's frame of reference, loosely speaking—through which he views the outside world.

A Restricted Window. This suggests immediately that one's view is restricted—he cannot see what is happening in back of him, above, to the sides, and so forth. One obviously cannot be ubiquitous and therefore his view is inevitably limited. But there is another restriction that he can overcome to an extent—the *size* of the window. We all have our "narrownesses"—our areas of naiveté. I, for example, was born and reared in a suburb. Suppose you are a country boy and we go out to a farm. We would share the same environment but I would expect that your stimuli and evoked sets would greatly outnumber mine. You would have the preparation, the memory content, to make so much more significance out of the experience than I.

But I have the capacity to learn. Given the time and provided I have the motivation I can acquire some of your sophistication. In short I can *expand* my window.

Stained-Glass Window. Not only is one's window frame restricted (but expandable largely at his will) but it also does not contain a pane of clear glass. It is rather like a stained-glass church window with various, peculiarly shaped, tinted, and refracting lenses. In one's frame of reference these lenses are his experiences, biases, values, needs, emotions, aspirations, and the like. They may all be distorting media to an extent but are we powerless to overcome these distortions? Hardly, but let us establish one point first.

Does anyone grow up with a clear window? Can anyone be without bias, for example? Quite unlikely, for everyone had to be born at a particular time and in a particular place. Thus he was exposed to particular people and situations all of whom and which taught him *special* lessons regarding values, customs, mores, codes, and so on.

But again man has viability and the capacity to adjust and compensate—he can *clarify* his window. A pencil in a glass of water appears to bend abruptly but if one *understands* something about the nature of refraction he can compensate for the distortion, aim at where the pencil appears not to be, and hit it. So it is more profoundly with a man himself—if he can *understand himself* he can *compensate* for his distorted frame of reference and, in effect, clarify his window.

ADDITIONAL READING

Borden, George A. *An Introduction to Human-Communication Theory.* Dubuque, Iowa: William C. Brown, 1971.
A brief introduction to a diverse body of theories of communication. Borden specifically surveys theories in the areas of communication process and model construction, selective perception, cognitive processes, and symbolization.

Brehm, Jack, and Arthur Cohen. *Explorations in Cognitive Dissonance.* New York: John Wiley & Sons, 1962.
A critical evaluation of the empirical data and research methodology supporting Festinger's theory of cognitive dissonance. The authors include the results from thirteen of their research studies, emphasizing the importance of commitment and choice to the arousal of dissonance. Implications of the theory are related to conflict and decision-making theories, personality dynamics, attitude change, desegregation, and indoctrination processes.

Brown, Roger. *Social Psychology.* New York: Free Press, 1965.
An explanation of language origin—from childish babbling and lallation to discovery of words—in chapters six and seven.

Cronkhite, Gary. *Persuasion: Speech and Behavioral Change.* Indianapolis, Ind.: Bobbs-Merrill, 1969.
A discussion of the psychological balance and dissonance theories of Heider, Osgood

and Tannenbaum, Festinger, Brown, McGuire, Rosenburg, Fishbein, Rokeach, and Katz in chapter three. Models accompany the explanations.

Festinger, Leon. *A Theory of Cognitive Dissonance.* Evanston, Ill.: Row-Peterson, 1957.
Cognitive dissonance as a tension-producer and motivator of behavior. Festinger studies the types of dissonance-reducing behaviors and their effects as efforts to achieve psychological homeostasis.

Heider, Fritz. "Attitudes and Cognitive Organization." *Journal of Psychology* 21 (1946):107–112.
One of the earliest psychological theories of attitude change. Heider's balance theory explains how an individual relates his attitudes to a second individual and to an object of judgment.

Maslow, Abraham H. *Motivation and Personality.* New York: Harper & Row, 1954.
A systematic theory of motivation and personality. Among the topics discussed are a theory of motivation, basic human needs—their instinctive nature and hierarchical operation—and self-actualization.

Osgood, Charles E., and Percy H. Tannenbaum. "The Principle of Congruity in the Prediction of Attitude Change." *Psychological Review* 62(1955):42–55.
A presentation of research data to verify a general theory of attitude change. Using a semantic differential for measurement, Osgood and Tannenbaum accommodate the original attitude toward the source of the message, the original attitude toward the concept evaluated by the source, and the nature of the evaluative assertion (the operational definition of attitude).

"I don't know what you mean by 'glory,'" Alice said.

Humpty Dumpty smiled contemptuously. "Of course you don't—till I tell you. I meant 'there's a nice knock-down argument for you!'"

"But 'glory' doesn't mean 'a nice knock-down argument,'" Alice objected.

"When I use a word," Humpty Dumpty said, in rather a scornful tone, *"it means just what I choose it to mean—neither more nor less."*

"The question is," said Alice, *"whether you can make words mean so many different things."*

"The question is," said Humpty Dumpty, *"which is to be master—that's all."*
—Lewis Carroll

4. SELF-EXPRESSION

OBJECTIVES In this chapter we ask you to do the following:

1. Recognize that words are symbols of human experiences and are not the experiences themselves.

2. Identify the elements of your own experiences that you have abstracted and associated with certain words.

3. Determine the degree to which words stimulate your recall of attitudes and emotional reactions to your experiences.

4. Practice using various levels of the "ladder of abstraction" to identify elements of your experience for others.

5. Analyze the power of word labels to direct personal behavior.

6. Consider language vocabulary and structure as factors that limit your thought capacity.

As you begin this chapter, continue trying to recognize the ways in which your experiences have shaped your self-concept; your attitudes, values, and beliefs; and the patterns that you have imposed on the events occurring around and inside you. Remember that you communicate from a unique point of view—your own way of looking at the world—and try to expand your observations to consider how you express your feelings, experiences, and goals.

Intrapersonal communication is the basis from which you attempt to make meaning for yourself and to share your experiences and information with other human beings. But it is important to realize that these attempts involve words and gestures that are not the experiences or bits of information themselves. Because you can't hand precise internal experiences of your world to others, you select and send them *symbols* (verbal and nonverbal representations of your individual judgments about reality that help others reconstruct these events or ideas in their minds). These symbols, then, operate somewhere between the stimulus events and the perceptions and cognitions of the people monitoring the symbols. Understanding the effect that word symbols have on people involves looking at the relationships between words and the objects they name, at the relationships between words and their human users, and at the nature of human language learning and use. If you have not considered what complex associations and relationships you encounter every time you use words to talk to yourself or others, this chapter may hold some surprises.

WORDS AND "THINGS"

What are we doing when we use words? We are using them as tools by which we relate to our worlds. We name things, explain processes, and give directions; we read about events as they occur, or we find accounts of them in textbooks as they are recorded; we write letters to maintain contact with those distant from us. Almost every important relationship we establish with ourself or with others is based in language; even our judgments are expressed in words. *Good* expresses a judgment, not an object, although we may hold the "good" object in our hands, we can never hold the word *good*.

Word symbols are the basis of human society. Is this a staggering claim? Perhaps they are, but consider the plight of the person who can not use the recorded knowledge of past generations as a basis for exploring new territory or sending ideas, thoughts, or discoveries to others at a distance. We learn from people in generations past (just as we teach those in generations to come) because symbols record human experience. However, the benefits of continuity across time that come from symbols should not overshadow the fact that *symbols are not the people, places, or ideas, but rather the external, shared representations of internal, individual human experiences of the people, places, and ideas.*

LANGUAGE AND EXPERIENCE

If a language is to meet the needs of a complex and rapidly changing society, it must supply a relatively small body of words that are capable of naming many experiences and of changing to accommodate new developments. The vocabulary must be small enough that native speakers can acquire common words, and large enough that it can describe the vast range of human experience. To show this flexibility in language, list as many different activities as you can think of that the word *sports* covers. To demonstrate further how a single word includes a lifetime of separate experiences, consider how a child entering grade school, completing high school, graduating from college, and, as an adult, choosing to become a teacher comes to know the term *teacher*. Obviously, we make our words correspond to what we learn about our world.

We not only use finite language to express an infinite range of experiences but also constantly change vocabularies. Words drop out of use as we no longer need them to identify outmoded objects or ideas, and we add words as we need to name new discoveries or processes. Before the electronic communication revolution, the terms *radio*, *television*, and *film* did not exist. More recently the vocabularies of the space program and electronic data processing have grown as rapidly as their discoveries have assumed importance. We should not take such flexibility in language to mean success in adapting, for often we do not know what internal experiences another person is referring to with a particular word choice. Nor should we blame confusion for our failure to provide a vocabulary with a specific word to correspond to every experience. We certainly could never master such a language. Without judgment, we note that this is a dilemma of human languages.

> *How long a time lies in one little word!*
>
> *—William Shakespeare*

Begin thinking about the language of your daily life. The word *chair* certainly is not what you are sitting on as you read this paragraph, just as the word *dog* will never bite. But given a room full of furniture, you are not apt to pick up a lamp when you have been asked to carry a chair. In a pet shop, you probably will not call the parakeet a dog. Throughout your life, you have had countless experiences with many different animals called *dogs*, pieces of furniture called *chairs*, buildings called *schools*, and people called *teachers*. Each experience has its own set of unique characteristics.

Figure 4-1

But you cannot observe all the characteristics of each event. Instead, you select its essential characteristics, store them in your mind as essential to represent the event, and assign a word symbol to name every future event with the same essential characteristics. I. A. Richards has named this mental process *conceptual abstraction*.

Some words clearly identify a specific event—i.e., the signing of the Declaration of Independence. Other words encompass a large number of objects, people, or ideas without specific reference to any one of them—i.e., drivers of red cars. Words that name a specific event are termed *concrete*. Words referring to a large class of events are called *abstract*. Words are more or less abstract, depending on the number of elements they represent out of the specific experience to be conveyed. Scholars have described the abstraction process as a ladder, with each step or level upward moving away from the actual event and eliminating some of its defining characteristics. They generally include the following levels in a diagram of the process:

Level 1:   The occurrence of the actual event (all characteristics are present).
Level 2:   The event as perceived by a human nervous system (only those characteristics that the senses monitor are included).
Level 3:   The labeling of the event with a word symbol (only the named characteristics are considered).
Level 4 to ∞:
           The classification of the event with other events having the same characteristics.

The higher and more abstract you become, the more events you include and the less you can say about each event. People often carry abstraction to the point of including so many events and excluding so many characteristics that they oversimplify complex issues. At this point, the issues have no meaning. Without knowledge of the concrete events referred to when someone says, "I'm sick of this whole economic mess!" it is easy for you to find such a statement completely meaningless.

<table>
<tr><td>**MAPS AND TERRITORIES**</td><td>Problems arise when you make abstractions because abstracting is a completely individualized human process. You choose to identify certain characteristics at each level of your ladder because they satisfy personal needs, wants, and goals. Words reveal more about your self-concept than they explain the objects you choose to describe. In comparison, think of verbal abstraction as an attempt to draw a map of a given territory. The territory is complete with all of its characteristics (lakes, trees, rocks, and roads) at level 1. At level 2, only those characteristics of the land perceived by the person about to draw the map are available. At level 3, the characteristics of the territory are further reduced to the elements actually depicted on the map. Maps can be more or less abstract, depending on the amount of territory they cover. Your chances of finding a street address in a given city</td></tr>
</table>

are much better if you use a city map than if you only have a map of the state, which lists the city as a small dot.

Do you remember the last time you gave someone directions over the telephone to find your home? Which landmarks did you include? Do you recognize these landmarks as the significant characteristics or elements of the route that you have abstracted during your many trips to and from your home? How well were you able to represent these characteristics to your friend? Did he or she follow your route directly to your home, or did the "brilliant red barn" marking the intersection at which to turn appear no more colorful than the six barns preceding it? As difficult as it is to guide others by concrete, observable landmarks, imagine trying to direct someone to be a "critical thinker" or a "free spirit." Even more difficult, imagine trying to decide whether and when that person succeeds.

We abstract more than geography when we make verbal maps. We select characteristics from the whole range of our experiences and identify them with words—none of which are "real" experiences. Just as *the abstract, verbal map is not the place* where we swim or visit friends, *the word is not the thing* that we have touched, tasted, felt, thought, smelled, or seen. To avoid physically carrying around every horse, table, chair, or experience, we store their characteristics and use word symbols to externalize our thinking. When we communicate a word to another person, we are not sharing our experience or meaning: we are asking that person to bring to consciousness the elements of experience that he or she has abstracted from events or objects labeled by that word. Unfortunately, we often assume that the person has abstracted the same elements of experience that we have and that we share a common meaning for the term. We must constantly remind ourselves that the words we use have no meanings; meanings exist only in the people who use the words. Consequently, if human thought operates through language, we must recognize that our knowledge has the inevitable ingredient of ambiguity.

WORDS AND USERS

Even when we recognize the potential for confusion in our use of language, we still have not begun to appreciate the tremendous power of words over all who use them. To this point in *Talk to Yourself*, we have considered ourselves in control of our language. We have the experiences; we abstract the elements; and we choose the word labels. But when we use words to describe our experiences, we reveal much more about our self-concept and life orientation than we reveal about people, objects, or events because we have abstracted those characteristics from our experiences that have met our needs, wants, and goals in the specific situations. In essence, our words give us away.

C. K. Ogden and I. A. Richards have diagramed this involvement of the individual in the context of the process of abstraction illustrated in figure 4–2. They define the *context* as the whole event, including all of its associations—psychological and external—from the individual's past experience. The *referent*—an object, person, or experience—stimulates the *thought or reference* to stored, past experiences of a similar nature, which are

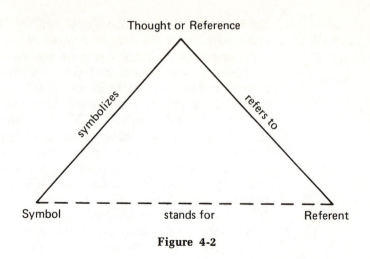

Thought or Reference

symbolizes   refers to

Symbol   stands for   Referent

Figure 4-2

expressed by a word *symbol*.[1] The important contribution that Ogden and Richards make in this model is their explanation of the different types of relationships among its elements. The two relationships indicated by unbroken lines—the relationship between symbol and reference and between reference and referent—are direct. Hearing a word symbol stimulates the thoughts or references in past experience that we have associated with that symbol. Conversely, the associated reference of similar experiences is stimulated in the presence of a referent. But the third relationship (the important one for our discussion)—that relationship between the symbol and the referent drawn with a broken line—is indirect. There is no predictable, constant relationship between the symbol and the referent—between the word and the thing. We will experience much difficulty with this relationship if we assume that words can have "correct" definitions. Because the reference associations of real people are unique and because they are formulated in a variety of contexts to meet individual needs and goals, any given word can hold multiple meanings for a person. The use of the same set of word symbols by different people can never stimulate the same reference sets or the same referent experiences. This is a property of language that is not to be praised or condemned, but rather to be remembered.

To test how clearly or ambiguously you are communicating, try Journal Exercise 5 at the back of the book.

Words express even more than the characteristics that we have abstracted from our experiences; they stimulate our recall of the attitudes and judgments that we have experienced in past situations. Words that we have read or heard in conversations with others have the power to trigger our emotional responses from past experiences.

Do you need proof of this power? To see how words evoke emotional responses, complete Exercise 20.

From this exercise, you can recognize the capacity of language to store elements of your experience and to stimulate your recall of attitudes and

[1] C. K. Odgen and I. A. Richards, *The Meaning of Meaning* (London: Routledge and Kegan Paul, 1923), p. 11.

Exercise 20

**Symbols,
Attitudes,
and Judgments**

The attitudes that you have acquired in abstracting from experience should surface readily when you see the following word symbols in this group exercise. Do you get positive (+), negative (−), or neutral (0) feelings when you read or hear them? Indicate your *immediate* response to each word in the list. Then write in a synonym (or referent) that describes your response for each word.

Word symbol	+ 0 −	Synonym
1. Power		
2. Organization		
3. Progress		
4. Pollution		
5. Peace		
6. Liberation		
7. Patriotism		
8. Communism		
9. Politician		
10. Radical		
11. Reactionary		
12. Wiretapping		
13. Sex		
14. Homosexual		
15. Marriage		
16. Commune		
17. Mother		
18. Atheist		

Total your positive responses, negative responses, and neutral responses. Are nine or more of your responses either positive or negative? Do you need further proof that words cause you to recall not only past experiences but also attitudes and emotions operating during those experiences?

Have your meanings for any terms changed recently (within the past five years)? What caused the change? Compare your responses with those of others in your class. Do the responses vary for different people? Are they ever the same? What are the referents (the particular persons, places, or things) you think of when you take in the words? Now identify ten additional key words in your vocabulary and value system.

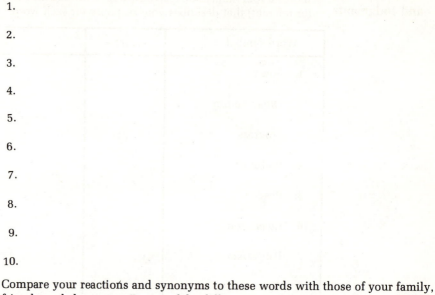

1.

2.

3.

4.

5.

6.

7.

8.

9.

10.

Compare your reactions and synonyms to these words with those of your family, friends, and classmates. Do any of the differences in reactions or referents surprise you?

Have you ever before analyzed the associations you make with these terms?

judgments about the experience. What additional influence do your words have on your behavior? You allow words to direct your behavior in many ways, or you assume that your words will dictate the behavior of others. In naming products or in writing the advertising copy to sell those products, admen behave as if they think that labels have some mystical power to guarantee the sale. How pretentious it is of the manufacturers to call a face cream Miracle Lotion! But imagine how many people are tempted to buy the product for the effects that the label promises. Do manufacturers of cars named Mustang, Pinto, Cougar, Jaguar, Stingray, Matador, or Ambassador expect consumers to transfer to the products the qualities implied by their names? Apparently they do, or advertising campaigns would change.

Of far greater concern are the word labels that you impose on others and on yourself. By calling someone a chauvinist, feminist, liberal, conservative, bigot, or intellectual, you classify him or her. No matter what else that person does or believes, you will select future perceptions and rationalize any new information to meet the expectations of your stereotype. When you label people negatively, you seldom allow them to redeem themselves. But if you are constantly labeling others, are they not also labeling and limiting you? What are some of the labels that others have used to identify you? Do you find yourself accepting their labels and conforming to their expectations?

Exercise 21

"I Am" Declarations

For this written exercise, keep a record of the times you say, "I am," in the next twenty-four hours. What follows after you say, "I am"? Whenever you say, "I am tired . . . grouchy . . . lonely . . . depressed," do you resemble a tired, grouchy, lonely, or depressed person? Can you change your feelings by changing your verbal labels? When you find yourself committing your language and thought to being tired or lonely, reverse your commitment and announce that you are happy, hopeful, or feeling fine. You can meet this commitment by internalizing your label and living up to it. Record any changes in verbal commitments and behavior along with your "I am" statements.

I am

I am

I am

I am

I am

I am

The labels that you use for yourself work in the same manner. Studies of the statements that individuals make about themselves have returned some interesting results. People who have a tendency to say, "That really eats me," or "Boy, that makes me sick to my stomach," are prone to suffer more from ulcers than people who avoid such language commitments. Similarly, people who constantly complain, "I'm tired," or "I'm worn out," seem to suffer more from fatigue than those who avoid these expressions.

Exercise 22

Labeling

In this group exercise, look at figures 4-3 to 4-8.

1. Quickly select a word that labels the individual in the picture according to your perception; write that label in the space provided. Do you really believe that each person is like your first impression? Are your labels as limiting as the pictures?

2. Explain to others in your group or class why you gave each one a particular label and what you perceive each to be doing.

3. Compare your labels with those of others in the class.

4. Find a picture of yourself or a close friend (not a posed shot).

5. Bring it to class and have classmates label the person pictured.

6. How accurate are their labels?

Figure 4-3

Stock, Boston

Figure 4-4

Stock, Boston

82   **Self-Expression**

Figure 4-5

Owen Franken, Stock, Boston

Figure 4-6

Burk Uzzie, Magnum

Figure 4-7

Alex Webb, Magnum

Figure 4-8

Magnum

TOWARD MORE EFFECTIVE LANGUAGE USE

Knowing the intrapersonal communication problems that language creates, can we make language a better or more reliable vehicle for carrying our ideas? The general semanticists, scholars who study the relationships between language, thought, and behavior, answer in the affirmative. They claim that most language problems stem not from the words themselves, but from attitudes about using the words. Therefore, a change in attitudes and an awareness of language operation should produce a corresponding change in communication effectiveness and satisfaction. Alfred Korzybski, founder of the discipline, outlines three principles of word-symbol operation:

1. The map is not the territory; the word is not the thing. A symbol must never be considered the nonverbal happening, idea, or person that it represents.

2. Be aware of the levels of abstraction. Whatever you may say about an event, you can never say it all.

3. Nothing is identical. Avoid using the word *is* to connect subjects and object modifiers.

Following these three principles, we can approach personal use of word symbols just as we would any empirical science. Korzybski also argues that we need to replace *intensional*, intellectual, or abstract definitions of people and events with *extensional*, factual, concrete material. Extensional refers to what we can examine visually, while intensional is concerned with the mental image, the idea, or the thought processes. He urges staying on the lower levels of the abstraction ladder, supplying the "where," "why," "what," "when," "who," "how," and "which one" for any experiences that we decide to share. As message senders, we need to choose words that allow others to reconstruct our internal reality. As a final suggestion, he urges us as listeners, watchers, or readers to try to discover the message elements the sender's words refer to, or at least to acknowledge the differences in the separate experiences labeled by the same words.

WORDS, LANGUAGE, AND LANGUAGE LEARNING

Understanding the problems of identifying concrete references to abstract words, and practicing the suggestions proposed by the general semanticists, should improve our ability to express internal experiences. But it is only the beginning in the investigation of language as an expressive tool in intrapersonal communication. Language behavior cannot be measured simply in words. Language influences communication behavior in much more extensive ways than is revealed by an explanation of the effects of words on the events they label (objects, people, and feelings) and on their human users. Analyzing a person's behavior as he or she uses or learns to use language leads to questions of how language is learned and, once it is learned, of what forms of behavior it directs.

We need to consider further what it is that we know when we learn a language and how this learning influences (that is, facilitates and/or hinders) our ability to express an intrapersonal experience. Research in the science of language and language problems (linguistics) is uncovering important information about the impact of language on our mental processes.

Language learning includes perceiving and producing the set of separate sounds that we combine to make the words of a given language. Babies begin this process with their early babbling of "da-das," "ma-mas," and "bye-byes." They continue adding sounds and words to identify objects and people in their environment, often receiving reinforcement from the people they name and toys or cookies for the objects they identify. By the age of two, children string words together, making simple two-word sentences—sentences that they may never have heard before, practiced in an English class, or read about in a grammar book. Equally important, children learn to understand sentences—verbal commands or requests—many of which they have never heard before. Rather than learning specific sentences, the children appear to learn rules or structural patterns—the grammar of sentences. Children of normal intelligence learn these rules for using the language before they reach age six. As evidence of further language development, children use the words of their vocabulary to create sentences that other speakers of their language understand. Such "creativity" remains with us as adults, enabling us to generate never-before-used sentences for others, who likewise understand the words as sentences of the language.

Among the theorists attempting to explain how the child acquires knowledge of language are Jean Piaget and Noam Chomsky.[2] Although their research methods and data differ, each agrees that human beings have a unique, innate capacity for acquiring a language.

You should consider the operation of these learned sentence structural patterns (or rules), beyond recognizing them as grammar models. Investigations are currently focusing on whether people can think outside of language. If they cannot think without language, how do structural rules restrict ways of viewing the world? Before continuing with the discussion of language structure and its implications, test your own knowledge of sentence structure rules with the following written exercise.

Exercise 23

Extending Sentences with Detail

As the following sentence is extended by phrases added to it, you can observe one aspect of the "creative" characteristic of language. Note that the sentence remains recognizable as a grammatical sentence.

The girl goes to school.
The girl *with the ponytail* goes to school.
The *five-year-old* girl *with the ponytail* goes to school.
The *five-year-old* girl *with the ponytail* goes to school *every day*.
The *five-year-old* girl *with the ponytail* goes to school *every day unless she is ill*.
The *five-year-old* girl *with the ponytail whose brother is in my class* goes to school *every day unless she is ill*.

Have you heard, read, or studied this set of sentences before? Do you recognize them as grammatically correct constructions of the English language? Although the last sentence is twenty-three words long, it should be judged just as grammatical as the original sentence of five words.

Demonstrate your own language creativity by expanding the following sentences with five additional phrases.

The bird flew to the tree.

[2] The specific research questions, methods, and conclusions can be found in the following sources: Noam Chomsky, *Aspects of the Theory of Syntax* (Cambridge, Mass.: MIT Press, 1965), and Jean Piaget, *The Language and Thought of the Child* (New York: Meridan, 1955).

The boy lives in a house.

Compare your sentences with those of others in your class. Did any of you generate the same set? Are they grammatically correct?

Another concern of the linguist is the question of how language participates in the thought process. According to the theorist Benjamin Lee Whorf, our thinking is structured by our culture; the most significant component of culture is language. Studying this hypothesis of "linguistic relativity," many scholars have reached this conclusion:

> Each language creates a special plight to which the individual must adjust. The human plight is in no sense universal save in this fact: that however different the language may be, it has certain common problems with which to deal—time, space, quantity, action, state, etc. But each language handles these problems differently and develops special ways of communicating. These ways of communicating create special needs, special responses, and lead to the development of special modes of thinking.[3]

Words are not simply strung together, one following another. We combine words of particular types or classes, which our schools teach us to call nouns, noun phrases, verbs, verb phrases, and so on, in a particular order (through the rules of syntax) to produce sentences that other native speakers of the language can recognize. A simple declarative sentence generally begins with a subject or noun phrase and then identifies the verb phrase, either an action or a condition of the subject.

[3] John B. Carroll and Joseph B. Casagrande, "The Functions of Language Classifications in Behavior," in Alfred G. Smith, *Communication and Culture: Readings in the Codes of Human Interaction* (New York: Holt, Rinehart & Winston, 1966), p. 491.

$$\frac{Helen}{noun\ phrase} + \frac{laughed.}{verb\ phrase} = sentence$$

Once we learn this sentence pattern, we can substitute other words of the same classes in the pattern. Instead of "Helen," perhaps "Laurie," "Renee," "Aunt Jane," or "our neighbor" functions as the subject. Word substitutions from the class of verbs or verb phrases might change the action from "laughed" to "ran," "drove," or "skipped."

For another example, to produce a simple question sentence, we learn a pattern that inverts the order of the declarative sentence. We change

$$\frac{Robert}{noun\ phrase} + \frac{was\ here.}{verb\ phrase} = declarative\ sentence$$

to

$$\frac{Was}{verb} + \frac{Robert}{noun\ phrase} + \frac{here?}{particle} = question\ sentence$$

Linguists are concerned whether the learned structures of language behavior also channel the thought process. Investigate parts of this theory yourself by discussing language problems with any of your classmates or friends who speak English as their second language. Ask them in which language they do their thinking—in English or their native language. Are there words or ideas from their native language that have no English equivalents? What is "normal" word order for different types of sentences in their language? When they have reached a conclusion in their thinking in their native language, are they able to convey these thoughts with an English translation? Relate their answers to your experience in speaking English. If you have no name for an idea or process, does that mean that you cannot discover the idea or process?

> . . . whatever we may say an object "is," it is not,
> because the statement is verbal, and facts are not.
>
> —Korzybski

After centuries of technological progress and increased educational opportunities for all, we still cannot handle our language. The technological revolution of the twentieth century has given us the capability to reach or contact all areas of the world, but this only increases our personal communication problems. Our educational systems annually graduate a number of students who cannot use language as a tool. Many have problems with reading, writing, and speaking. Perhaps the reason that we fail lies in our approach.

In addition to the new words that we can easily add to our language, we need a new attitude about using our language. We must remember that our common medium of language identifies a diversity of values, experiences, and, of course, meanings.

Exercise 24

Abstract Terms

The objectives of this group exercise are to (1) identify elements that you have abstracted from your personal experience that are labeled by a word symbol, and (2) select resource material that presents concrete examples to clarify your abstract term.

In the exercise, you will select an abstract word or phrase (like love, freedom, or beauty) naming a quality or attribute that you particularly value. Your goal is to communicate that abstract idea by using concrete terms and references that will allow the class audience to understand the unique meaning you associate with that term.

1. *Introduction:* In a three-to-five-minute speech, identify the term and briefly explain its place in your value system.

2. *Content:* Find at least three selections of prose, drama, or poetry (preferably a combination of all three) that explain or clarify your abstract term. For example, in a speech developing the concept of freedom, you could use quotations from a representative Civil War spokesperson, from the works of a political theorist, and from a poem dealing with freedom as its general subject. Your reading from these selections should take up to three minutes. Don't hesitate to include references to personal incidents.

3. *Conclusion:* Conclude your presentation by summarizing the concrete images that the prose, drama, and poetry readings and personal narratives have provided to communicate the abstract term.

4. *Evaluation:* Describe and evaluate your communication behavior in the following categories: preparation, presentation, evaluation, and re-presentation. Refer to page 20 for format.

SUMMARY

Words are expressive tools of human communication, the external evidence of our intrapersonal information processing. They symbolize our experiences, but they cannot be those experiences. We share our experiences by using word symbols, from which others attempt to reconstruct our reality. Learning a language involves learning a relatively small body of words to represent the full range of human experiences. Consequently, we classify similar experiences and use words to represent both their common characteristics and our attitudes toward the experiences. This process, called conceptual abstraction, means that ambiguity is an inevitable component of language. Following the prescriptions of the general semanticists, we should describe our experiences with the most concrete terms possible.

Learning words is only one part of understanding language. Many linguists are investigating the child's capacity to acquire language. Others are researching the interaction of language with thought. They recognize that words are not randomly strung together. However, it remains to be proven whether language structure limits the potential of human thought or structures intrapersonal communication.

SUPPLEMENTARY READING

In his article, "Limiting Structures of Language and Culture," Richard Marsh proposes making visible the consequences of English language structures and cultural biases. He asserts that the structures and biases create an "invisible prison" that determines how we perceive and identify our worlds; this "invisible prison" causes us to focus on certain events and to ignore others. Marsh reinforces and extends the claims that we have developed in this chapter, and he particularly supports the idea that studying language complexities beyond semantic properties is necessary.

LIMITING STRUCTURES OF LANGUAGE AND CULTURE

Richard P. Marsh

A person in jail who doesn't know he's in jail is doubly a prisoner. In a sense, every one of us is in jail without realizing it. That's because the prison in which we are trapped is invisible, and since it's invisible, we're not aware that we're trapped. The first step toward our release is to become aware of the prison.

Actually, we're trapped in two prisons, both of them invisible. The first of these is the structure of language itself. The second is the effect of our culture on the way we live. Let's have a look at these two prisons. Perhaps if we become aware of them we can improve our chances of escaping from them.

First of all, let's look at the structure of language, not from a narrow linguistic point of view but from a broader metalinguistic point of view. Why do you like people to remember your name? Perhaps one reason is that if they know your name they are more apt to notice you. People see things they have words for; they ignore things that they have no words for. Somebody has suggested that romantic love is largely the creation of poets—if there had been no love poetry, ninety-five percent of the people who fall in love wouldn't fall in love because they wouldn't have the words for it.

Advertising is based on this principle. The advertiser drills in the name of his product so that the customer will notice it. When you walk through a supermarket, Campbell's soups spring out at you. Sloppy Joe's soups recede into the background, even though their label may be every bit as vivid.

What we see is determined by what we say about what we see. We see what we have names for; we ignore what we have no names for. At any rate, this is the hypothesis of Benjamin Lee Whorf, Edward Sapir, and Alfred Korzybski. Noting that

Reprinted from *Teaching General Semantics* by permission of the International Society for General Semantics.

different languages chop up the world in different ways by imposing a different verbal grid structure, so to speak, on the underlying processive flow, they hypothesize that this may affect the way in which people notice, perceive, and experience the world. In other words, they suggest, people who speak different languages live in different worlds. . . .

English is one of the Indo-European languages. It is a superb language, but like every language, it has its built-in strengths and limitations. One of the characteristic features of the Indo-European languages is that they rely heavily on the subject-predicate structure. We say, for example, "The wave rolled along the ocean and crashed against the beach." This implies that there is a solid something known as a "wave" which performs an act known as "rolling" and "crashing." What it ignores is the fact that the wave *is* the rolling and the crashing—no rolling and no crashing, no wave. A wave is not a thing, it is a movement.

As Stuart Chase explains in *The Power of Words,* the Hopi Indian language used a much more sensible word for the wave, a word that can be translated into something like the English word "slosh." Slosh is a better fit than wave because it has built into it some of the feeling of movement that actually occurs in a wave. The word "wave" stops the process, much as we stop the process of a living cell when we kill it, slice it, mount it on a slide, and stain it so that we can look at it under a microscope.

We say, "The dancer danced." But this ignores the fact that the dancing *is* the dancer and the dancer *is* the dancing. If there's no dancing, there's no dancer. We say "The flame burned." But the flame *is* the burning. No burning, no flame. No flame, no burning. Wave, dancer, and flame are not things that move. They are movements. The Indo-European languages rely heavily on substantives; that is, nouns, pronouns, etc.—words like wave, dancer, flame. We like to have nouns connected with verbs—things or essences connected with movements or processes—ignoring the fact that the thing and the process are inseparable.

Consider the falling of the rain. In English we say, "It is raining," seldom stopping to look for the "it" that rains. We say, "The light flashed," ignoring the fact that the light *is* the flashing and not a separate thing. The Hopi Indians manage this better. They have a word, as Stuart Chase points out, something like "Flash!"—a word that is neither a verb nor a noun, but a little of both. In English and other Indo-European languages, because of their reliance on substantives coupled with predicates, we keep introducing various "ghostly entities" that flash, rain, dance, etc. We like "things" and "essences" because our language is built that way.

If something is cold, we look for the "cold" *in* it, assuming that, because we are able to use the word "cold" as a noun, therefore cold must be a thing. Scientists, however, know better. They say we should start with heat. Heat, they tell us, is a happening—a process, a relationship, a set of vibrations. Cold is merely the absence of this happening. It is not a thing in and of itself, the way a billiard ball is a thing in and of itself. So, according to the Whorf-Sapir-Korzybski hypothesis, our emphasis on subjects and predicates and our fondness for substantives tends to cause us to miss the process view basic to modern science and communication theory. It encourages us to see a static world of unchanging things. We say, "Boys will be boys," but what we forget is that boys will also be men some day and, in some of the more experimental subcultures of our society, boys will sometimes be girls. As a result we tend to perceive our universe as made up of billiard ball objects going through a set of mechanical movements.

As Stuart Chase reminds us, all languages, including the Indo-European languages, contain terms of "cosmic grandeur." What, after all, is referred to by such words as "reality," "matter," "substance," "cause," "energy," "space," "time," etc.? Look at your watch. You can see the hand, the stem, and so on, and if you were to open it you would see the mechanism inside. But you cannot see "time" as such. "Time" is a term of "cosmic grandeur." All you can see when you look at your watch is motion and relationship. . . .

Push an object off your table. Watch the object drop to the floor. What have you seen? You have seen the movement of your hand in contact with the object, you have seen the glide of the object along the table, and you have seen the movement of the object from the table to the floor. You have not seen the *cause* for the falling of the object. There is nothing to which you can point and say, "This is the cause." You can point only to the hand, the object, the table, and the various movements involved. "Cause" is a term of cosmic grandeur that refers to something in one's head rather than to something in physical reality.

And yet most of us in the Western World are firmly convinced that every effect has a cause and that we can, with a little effort, designate the cause. Most of us are convinced that we know what reality is and what matter is. The existence of such things as time, space, and energy seems self-evident. Still, none of these things has solid existence in the sense that a billiard ball has solid existence. The metalinguistic theory of language asserts that the use of these words tends to determine the way in which we perceive and experience the universe.

An illuminating comparison can be made between an Indo-European language like English and an oriental language such as Chinese. English makes much more use of the verb "to be" and its various forms than does Chinese. Look at your pencil. You may say of the pencil, "It is yellow" and "It is hard." By means of the word "is" you connect "yellowness" and "hardness" with the pencil. It is as though you had said "The pencil *has* yellowness, and it *has* hardness." Now point to the "yellowness" and the "hardness" which the pencil "has." You will find the yellowness and hardness have no existence apart from the pencil and apart from your own nervous system. They are subjective experiences resulting from a set of relationships. They are also, perhaps, the result of the subject-predicate form of the typical English sentence.

The Chinese, however, do not place nearly so heavy a stress on subjects and predicates. The Chinese are much less apt to construct sentences based on words like the English verb "to be." Therefore, according to the metalinguists, they are less likely to suppose that qualities such as yellowness, hardness, and other attributes can exist apart from the object to which we impute them.

Another difference between English and Chinese is that the use of "polar words" is much less characteristic of the latter than of the former. Look at a piece of chalk. Note its front end and its rear end. Note how easy it is to keep them separate in mind. Now break the chalk into two pieces. What has become of the front end and the rear end? The structure of the English language with its numerous pairs of opposites like front and rear, big and small, wet and dry, etc., makes it easy for us to think in terms of polar opposites. It seems natural for us to think of a piece of chalk or any other object as having "frontness" and "rearness"—a front end and a rear end—existing as separate things or entities. The oriental languages, however, are so constructed that it's more difficult to separate in your mind one quality from its opposite. In the oriental view, opposites are not opposed. They arise mutually, they are complementary.

The essential complementariness or unity of opposites is symbolized in Chinese culture by the yang-yin symbol. Night begins at high noon. Day begins at midnight. The difference between pain and pleasure is to some extent an opinion. The Chinese appear to be aware of this fact, perhaps because their language is multi-valued. English, on the other hand, is relatively two-valued. This may be one reason why Americans and other English-speaking people have difficulty being happy and sad, rational and passionate, active and passive, etc., at the same time without feeling divided against themselves. Convinced by the structure of their language that they should be either one thing or another but not opposite things at the same time, they begin to oscillate or dither. Subjectively, they feel the state of dithering as anxiety. . . .

In English grammar, "sit" is a verb. "Sit" (in the form of "sitting") is also a noun, as in the sentence "sitting is restful." Or, again, it may be an adjective, as in the expressions "sitting duck" and "Sitting Bull." It is nonsense to separate the action, the thing, and the quality in this way, but we do so, thanks to the structure of our language, and consequently we create for ourselves a billiard-ball world.

This is not to say that a knowledge of English grammar is useless. A person with a mastery of English grammar is in a favored position. As far as I know—although I've had no direct experience in the matter—he will not get into heaven any sooner than a person without that knowledge. But he will be admitted into certain social circles, and he will be eligible for certain jobs that would be forbidden to him without his knowledge of English grammar. English grammar is simply "the English way of saying the thing." There is nothing absolute or inherently correct about it. However, there is a communicative aspect to grammar. Not saying something "grammatically"—that is, not speaking English in the English way of speaking English—tends to call attention to itself and so to interfere with communication. . . .

The consequences of the linearities and polarities of English and other Indo-European languages are evident in certain psychological attitudes characteristic of Western man. Consider the contrast between the Western and the Oriental view of time. Instead of seeing time as something lineal like an arrow moving through space, the Oriental tends to see it as circular. This habit is reflected in such beliefs as reincarnation, the notion that the cosmic processes repeat themselves cyclically, etc. In the Western world we believe that opportunity knocks but once. Our state of mind is like that of a man standing on the brink of a stream waiting for a single fish to come along, anxiously holding on to the harpoon with which he expects to spear it, grimly ready in a now-or-never stance. Consequently, we are hurried, anxious, always planning, budgeting, computing, scheduling. The Orientals, by contrast, have developed more of a next-time-around attitude. What doesn't get done now can get done in some later incarnation, in some later re-cycling of the cosmic process. There are always more fish swimming downstream. Consequently, the Orientals are relatively serene and relaxed.

However, it is possible to overemphasize the destructive consequences of the structure of the English language. A language may be seen not only as an invisible prison but also as an invisible guide. Perhaps the lineal, sequential form of the Indo-European sentence and the Indo-European thought processes, as opposed to the more circular form of the Oriental thought processes, is one reason why we in the Western world are more goal-seeking than our companions in the Eastern Hemisphere. And our goal-seeking tendency may be one reason why we have accomplished more in the way of altering the physical environment, while the Orientals, except where they are Westernized like the Japanese, have been comparatively backward in technological matters.

So language can be looked at in two ways. It may be seen as an invisible prison causing us to experience the non-verbal world we inhabit in a distorted kind of way. Or it may be thought of as an invisible guide, leading our attention to various aspects of the universe so that we are able to develop certain kinds of more or less useful technologies and scientific systems.

Let us turn now to the culture concept. Culture, which is practically synonymous with language—or at least with the larger notion "communication" —also has this double quality. Culture, like language, is both an invisible prison and an invisible guide. By "culture" I don't mean going to the opera or to art galleries. I mean culture as it's used in expressions like "Western culture" or "Japanese culture." It's the way people do things, how they live together, interact, organize their lives. E. T. Hall calls it "the silent language." Just as spoken and written language tells us how to perceive the universe, how to chop it up into categories, so also the silent language of culture tells us how to see the world around us and especially the people in that world.

We all seem to have an almost instinctive sense of the "proper" distance to stand from people. However, it's not instinctive at all. Actually, it's something that we begin learning at birth and continue learning, unconsciously, for the rest of our lives. In every culture there is a sense of appropriateness in regard to how near and how far from other people one should stand. And this varies widely from culture to culture.

You may have heard it said of some foreigners that they seem "pushy" whereas others are "distant" or "aloof." Actually, this results from a misconception of what's happening. Foreigners whom we take to be pushy are not pushy at all. They merely come from a culture in which, as a matter of course, people stand rather close to one another. Similarly, other kinds of foreigners are not distant or aloof. They simply come from a culture in which it seems appropriate to stand at some distance from other people.

What it comes down to is that members of different cultures habitually divide up space in a characteristic kind of way that sets them apart from the members of other cultures.

The fascinating part about all of this is that the various members of the particular cultures don't realize that they have a characteristic way of dividing up space, a characteristic distance at which they stand from other people, a characteristic distance at which they build their houses from one another, a characteristic preference for certain kinds of spatial divisions.

In addition to these preferences about spatial division, preferences about temporal division also exist in different cultures. In other words, the members of different cultures divide up time in characteristic kinds of ways. Everyone has what appears to be an instinctive sense of when he is "on time" for an appointment and when he is "late." We seem to know, as though instinctively, how "late" we can be for particular appointments with particular people at particular points in the social pecking order without being offensive.

The way in which we divide up time, like the way we divide up space, is not instinctive however, but is a habit acquired from our experiences in a particular culture. You probably know some people who are always late and others who are irritatingly on time. The next time you are annoyed by one of these people you may want to meditate on the fact that the reason for their habitual-seeming lateness or their excessive on-timeness may be that they were reared in a different culture from yours—or even a different subculture.

In any case, standards of punctuality vary widely from culture to culture. Moreover, the members of any given culture or subculture tend to have an unerring sense of what is appropriate. It operates so automatically that it seems to be instinctive, although actually it is learned.

The ugly American—or, for that matter, the ugly Russian or the ugly Anything Else—is to a large extent a person who is unaware of these differing attitudes towards dividing up space and time.

The very important matter of dividing space and time in such a way that everyone within a particular culture feels comfortable is regulated by what E. T. Hall calls the *informal rule* of the culture. Now, a problem arises from the fact that, although the normal or average person within a culture follows these rules with great skill, he has no conscious knowledge of them. He is their prisoner without realizing that he is their prisoner. At the same time a person from another culture is their prisoner in a different sense. He is not only blissfully unaware of them, but he also lacks the unconscious grasp of them that guides the normal member of the culture. But, since even those who follow these rules do so unconsciously, the rules are difficult, if not impossible, to formulate clearly. Consequently, it becomes extremely difficult, if not impossible, to teach or to learn them in a deliberate, systematic, conscious way.

In addition to these informal rules, every culture has also developed a number of *formal rules*. These are the rules that tell us what to believe about God, how to feel about our country, whether or not one can marry his cousin without being guilty of incest, whether or not to split an infinitive, whether it is permissible to whistle in church, and so forth. They are the rules governing the ultimate values of the culture. Formal rules of this sort can be clearly stated, the normal member of the community is clearly conscious of them, but violation of them is out of the question. A good American just doesn't wipe his shoes on the "American flag even though, after all, it's just a piece of cloth." And even an atheist in a particular culture will avoid the extreme forms of what is considered blasphemy in that culture.

The members of a particular culture are the willing, conscious prisoners, so to speak, of the formal rules of the culture. The normal or average member of the culture considers the formal rules of that culture to be absolutely binding on his behavior. Yet there's nothing intrinsically superior or inferior in different metaphysical views of the world or in different attitudes toward marriage with one's cousin.

Culture, then, provides us with formal and informal rules for codifying and classifying reality and for communicating with each other. In the current slang, culture is the "games" we play, and of course the rules of any game are subject to change—if only we know that we are playing the game.

There is great value in culture to the extent that we see through it—see through the game, so to speak. Attempting as much as possible to see through the culture, through the game, through the assumptions embedded in this particular language—this is the way to break out of the invisible prison and transform it into a useful guide on our way toward achieving the human potential.

There are two main functions of education and the arts: (1) to teach the games so to speak, of one's culture—the rules for dividing space and time; (2) to teach one to see through the rules of one's culture. Unfortunately, however, education and the arts too often succeed in the former and fail in the latter. Nonetheless, both of these functions are indispensable. Young people must learn a language and absorb culture in order to become human. They must also transcend these in order to achieve their highest potentials.

We are all, at once, the beneficiaries and the victims of our culture and our language. They are the repository of whatever is beautiful and of whatever is monstrous in human invention. Without language and culture we are animals. With language and culture we may become something less than animals—we may become monsters—unless we have some insight into their workings and escape from the invisible prison in which they contain us.

There is a difference between the wisdom of the ages and the organized idiocy of the past. Language and culture are the vehicles for both of these. Whether they limit us in the form of invisible prisons, or lead us beyond ourselves in the direction of achieving our human potentials depends on how aware we are of what's happening to us. Keeping that awareness alive is an extremely difficult thing to do, but I think we all have to try.

Bibliography

Chase, Stuart, and Marian T. Chase. *The Power of Words.* New York: Harcourt Brace Jovanovich, 1954.

Hall, Edward T. *The Silent Language.* Garden City, New York: Doubleday, 1959.

ADDITIONAL READING

Brown, Roger. *Words and Things.* New York: Free Press, 1958.
    An explanation of language as an aspect of human behavior. Brown looks for its origin in children and traces its development into a tool for propaganda and advertising.

Chase, Stuart. *The Tyranny of Words.* New York: Harcourt Brace & World, 1938.

A popularized application of the principles of general semantics to the realms of philosophy, economics, law, logic, and politics.

Chomsky, Noam. *Aspects of the Theory of Syntax.* Cambridge, Mass.: MIT Press, 1965.
An explanation of the theory of transformational generative grammar. Chomsky probes the child's discovery of the deep and abstract theory of language, and he records the observable language "universals" that reflect the possibility of a common ability to acquire knowledge.

Fromkin, Victoria, and Rodman, Robert. *An Introduction to Language.* New York: Holt, Rinehart & Winston, 1974.
Information on the three main components of language—phonetics and phonology, semantics, and syntactics. This comprehensive introductory text further speculates on these questions: What is language? What do you know when you know a language? What is the origin of language? How do children acquire language?

Hayakawa, S. I. *Language in Thought and Action.* 2d ed. New York: Harcourt, Brace & World, 1964.
The thesis that language is the fundamental mechanism of human survival. First published as *Language in Action* in 1941, Hayakawa's text continues to offer situations from daily experiences to illustrate this thesis. He offers rules for mediating language-produced conflict through an extensional orientation.

———— (ed.) *The Use and Misuse of Language.* Greenwich, Conn.: Fawcett, 1962.
A collection of articles reprinted from *ETC.: Review of General Semantics.*

Johnson, Wendell. *People in Quandaries: The Semantics of Personal Adjustment.* New York: Harper and Brothers, 1946.
An explanation of social and individual problems through an analysis of language structure. This analysis verifies the hypothesis that "adequate behavior" requires an understanding that words represent only abstractions of experience with many details omitted. Exercises and concrete applications of general semantics for daily living make up this highly readable account.

————. *Your Most Enchanted Listener.* New York: Harper and Brothers, 1956.
A continuation of Johnson's thesis that human problems of adjustment originate in our inability to talk freely to ourselves and to recognize language as the thinking medium. He also explains how the symbol projects feelings back to the language user.

Korzybski, Alfred. *Science and Sanity: An Introduction to Non-Aristotelian Systems and General Semantics.* New York: International Non-Aristotelian Library Publishing Company, Science Press Printing Co., 1933.
A highly technical treatment of the consequences of symbolization. Korzybski rejects the principle of "identity" for that of "multiordinal terms." The "structural differential" identifies different levels of orders of abstractions (each level having different meanings and no general meanings) and illustrates the means by which one can achieve an extensional orientation. This is not a textbook for the beginning student.

Lee, Irving J. *Language Habits in Human Affairs.* New York: Harper and Brothers, 1941.
An introduction to the general semantics of Korzybski. Lee explains two premises: (1) human beings have difficulties in making accurate statements about themselves and their world, and (2) personal and social maladjustment is rooted in "false-to-fact" language habits. This text contains numerous cases of language abuse in daily speech.

Morris, Charles. *Signs, Language, and Behavior.* New York: George Braziller, 1955.
A detailed and critical evaluation of the syntactic, semantic, and pragmatic dimensions of language, as they influence personal and social behavior.

Ogden, Charles K., and Richards, Ivor A. *The Meaning of Meaning.* London: Routledge and Kegan Paul, 1923.
The "triangle of meaning." The major contribution of Ogden and Richards to the study of the influence of language on thought is the graphic representation that this triangle provides. It emphasizes the differences between our mental references to the characteristics of objects and events and the symbolic means by which we communicate these mental references.

Piaget, Jean. *The Language and Thought of the Child.* New York: Meridian, 1955.
The research questions, methods, and conclusions of studies that observe the emergence of language and the underlying cognitive development in children.

Whorf, Benjamin Lee. *Language, Thought, and Reality: Selected Writings of Benjamin Lee Whorf,* Edited by John Carroll. New York: John Wiley & Sons, 1956.
   Almost all of Whorf's papers on the hypothesis of "linguistic relativity." Two premises emerge: (1) all higher levels of thinking are dependent on language, and (2) the structure of the language we commonly use affects the manner in which we understand our environment.

I . . . have never been the same person alone that I am with people.
                                                                —*Philip Roth*

5. BEYOND THE WORLD OF INTRA

OBJECTIVES   In this chapter we ask you to do the following:

1. Realize that you never finish the process of intrapersonal communication.

2. Understand the changes that have taken place in you and accept changes in others.

3. Share your thoughts of self-concept with others.

4. Evaluate your interpersonal communication abilities.

In the beginning of this text we established that all communication relies on intrapersonal communication. You never really leave the world of intrapersonal communication because you always take yourself with you. But you do not create your self-concept by yourself; it is an integration of what you perceive in your communication with others. We do not intend to write a chapter on interpersonal communication, since that subject fills numerous books. Our interest here is in preparing you to make your internalized thoughts external, ready for two-way communication.

We have endeavored to give you a new frame of reference, but what you do with it is up to you. Have you ever heard art teachers exclaim, "No, no, don't rework the painting. Change the frame."? An experienced artist knows the hazards of improper framing. One bad frame can distort, cast shadows on, and give a false perspective to a good picture. Seeing a badly framed picture, the inexperienced individual might logically try to rework the picture on the canvas and risk ruining it. But if the picture is properly framed, it takes on the beauty, dimension, and clarity that the artist intended.

In the preceding four chapters we have tried to help you develop a new perspective on how you view yourself. You might already have an excellent self-portrait, but you may have framed it incorrectly because you thought that was the frame that others wanted or that was how they viewed you—forcing you to act as if you were something that you are not. Or you may have used a totally opaque frame that hid your self-portrait.

You need to watch what you are using to maintain your self-image. It's not enough to change just one area of thought; that would be like trying to take out one piece of a badly framed picture. You must open up all areas of thought. You need to place the entire range of your thinking in a new and truer frame of reference.

In the first four chapters you have been busy involving yourself with your self-concept. We have asked you questions and we have asked you to ask yourself questions. But we have not finished with our questioning process. Do you think that you are ready to share your new concept of self with someone? Do you really want someone to know who you are? Have you discovered yet who you are? What do you want out of interpersonal relationships?

ACCEPTING CHANGE IN YOURSELF AND OTHERS

The process of getting to know yourself is not an overnight project. It takes time and a willingness to want to know. If you ask the oft-repeated question, "Who am I?" then you should be willing to grapple with the task of soul-searching and self-disclosure. As the preceding chapters have explained, isolating your attitudes, values, and beliefs from the specific events or people associated with them is a difficult task. This time, as you look into the mirror, consider the images that appear to meet the expectations of your parents, friends, spouse, employer, or teachers. How do you change your communication behavior for the situations in which you encounter these people? What characteristics remain constant in any relationship that you experience? Also consider the image that you present in confronting new people and unfamiliar situations. (You may wish to include your responses to the preceding questions under miscellaneous journal entries at the back of the book.)

You should have witnessed changes in your self-image as people and situations around you have changed. You should feel differently since you have completed your self-concept collage and have had your beliefs challenged. Consequently, the notion of an unchanging self-concept is as erroneous as the idea that words convey the same meaning for all people. We hope that by now you realize that you are becoming a more honest and aware person as your perceptions of the world are given dimension and as you are learning to cope with personal problems. When you have reached the point of self-acceptance, you are ready to accept others. "When I accept myself as I am, I change, and when I accept others as they are, they change."

When you realize that all the problems of life are in you in some way, shape, or form, how can you get angry at them in someone else? How do you view other people? Do you see them as limited? Do not hastily label others as nonthinkers or dolts; wait until you begin to understand their circumstances before you evaluate them. There is an old Indian saying, "If you walked in your brother's moccasins a fortnight, you would know what makes him act as he does."

> To be nobody-but-yourself—in a world which is
> doing its best, night and day, to make you everybody
> else—means to fight the hardest battle which any
> human being can fight; and never stop fighting.
>
> —e.e. cummings

Remember that we asked you consciously to be aware of what you claimed for yourself when you said, "I am." Make the same kind of inventory when you say "he is" or "she is." Too often you see less than the "real" person because your qualities and perceptions have made you so shortsighted.

A student in a communications class went out to apply the axiom "Change your thought of yourself and you change your view of others." John used to run through a subway terminal to catch his train at night. Each evening he passed a man sitting on the ground with an empty cup and a handful of pencils. John usually threw in change every evening. One time as he started to get on his train, he realized that he had been seeing that man as a beggar. He stopped, ran back to the man, and said, "I just gave you a quarter, and I give to you frequently. I am sorry, but I have never taken your pencils. You see, I have been seeing you as a beggar, but you are a businessman. Please allow me to take my pencils." John was quite pleased that he had checked his thought about the man.

Three months later when John was dashing for his train, a man hailed him. John stopped, and the man who had been selling pencils before introduced himself. He thanked John for taking the time to stop and tell him that he saw the man as a businessman. He said, "No one ever told me I was anything but a beggar. I never saw myself as a businessman until you took the time to tell me. I went home and thought about it, and you are right. I am a businessman, and to prove it I opened this newsstand." This man was now selling newspapers, magazines, and assorted novels.

Think of it! You could improve many lives if you changed your negative view of people. By taking the time to share your thoughts, you help to shape someone else's self-concept.

A woman named Cynthia used to frequent a bakery, where she tried to avoid getting one salesclerk. But every time that her number came up, she got the acid-tongued woman who had little patience for someone asking, "Is that strawberry or raspberry inside your jelly rolls?" Cynthia had decided to quit going to that bakery; her encounter with this woman was so distasteful that it practically ruined her day. Her husband suggested to her that she change her view of this woman and be more friendly. "How can you be more friendly with a grizzly bear?" she retorted. But Cynthia decided to give it a try. Each time that she went into the bakery after that, she took the time to tell the woman how nice she looked or how much she appreciated her speedy service, and she would always wish the woman a good day. One day a couple of months later, Cynthia found herself alone in the bakery with this woman. The salesclerk confided that she had back and leg problems and that she was working at this job to earn enough money to have an operation. She found it difficult to be pleasant with people because she was in pain most of the time, and so she was grateful that Cynthia took the time to be friendly; most customers avoided her or were equally abrupt. The salesclerk eventually developed a more cheerful outlook toward her job and the people with whom she did business.

It is important in the self-actualizing process of intrapersonal communication to become aware of others while you are developing a new awareness of yourself. You might relate to the following account of a Chicago businessman. Jud observed eight people who regularly ate lunch together. He watched in amazement as everyone talked at once. No one seemed to listen to anyone else, and no one showed concern over the absence of response to their comments. When they returned to work, they all appeared to enjoy the experience and each other's company.

This may not seem like an example of intrapersonal communication, because the people were in the presence of others. Their self-orientation would make you wonder whether they were using intrapersonal or interpersonal communication, since they all appeared to be out for themselves, with no apparent interest in, concern for, or response to the others. To evaluate your interpersonal communication, complete Journal Exercise 6 at the back of the book.

Sharing with others is an important step in gaining interpersonal trust. Try the following group exercise to gain an awareness of sharing.

Exercise 25

Secret Sharing

In this class assignment, put a secret on a sheet of paper without signing your name and give the paper to your instructor. As your instructor reads the secrets aloud, how do you react? Were others in the class just writing down superficial secrets to get through the assignment? In your estimation, did anyone really reveal a secret? Keep in mind that perception is an individual thing. Could any of the secrets read aloud have pertained to you at some point in your experience?

A winter's day
In a deep and dark December;
I am alone,
Gazing from my window to the streets below
On a freshly fallen silent shroud of snow.
I Am A Rock,
I am an island.

I've built walls,
A fortress deep and mighty,
That none may penetrate.
I have no need of friendship; friendship causes pain.
It's laughter and it's loving I disdain.
I Am A Rock,
I am an island.

Don't talk of love,
But I've heard the words before;
It's sleeping in my memory.
I won't disturb the slumber of feelings that have died.
If I never loved I never would have cried.
I Am A Rock,
I am an island.

I have my books
And my poetry to protect me;
I am shielded in my armor,
Hiding in my room, safe within my womb.
I touch no one and no one touches me.
I Am A Rock,
I am an island.

And a rock feels no pain;
And an island never cries.

—Paul Simon

What do the words to this song by Paul Simon mean to you? Do they suggest anything about your self-concept? Do you believe that you can live away from others? Why? If you do not like yourself, you will build walls to hide or to protect what little you think you have. You will wear masks and play games, and you may never find out who you are, justifying your masks and games by saying, "I don't care." But you really do care.

If you want to get to know others and share with them, you must start with yourself. If you have been completing the exercises and adding to your journal, you are ready at this point to see why your self-concept is so important in interpersonal affairs. This culture seems increasingly to be

changing its emphasis from achievement to self-concept and self-expression. Your ability to understand yourself will be helpful in your interpersonal relationships. Today, employers are looking for individuals with a positive self-concept. The objective of many aptitude and personality tests is to measure how you view yourself. If you see yourself as incompetent, shy, and fearful, the chances are that not many employers would hire you, since they would have to take on the responsibility of trying to build your self-confidence. It is much easier to deal with those who have a sense of worth and feel that they have a contribution to make.

To develop and maintain effective relationships, you should have acquired certain skills in the intrapersonal processing. Ask yourself, "Do I know and trust myself?" If you do, you can probably know and learn to trust others. Ask, "Am I accurate and unambiguous in understanding myself?" If so, you can probably be accurate and unambiguous in understanding others.

If people do not seem friendly toward you, occasionally you should ask yourself whether you are really being friendly. Are you trustworthy, honest, thoughtful, grateful, and joyous? You should be expressing just as much in yourself the qualities that you look for in others.

Maybe the person that you have been dating has broken up with you, and you feel lonely and hurt. Perhaps you have moved to a new city, and you have not found a group of people with whom you feel comfortable. Your experience and your world are one, and you make this world by your thoughts and actions. Problems often seem to arise out of external circumstances, but the fears, doubts, and angry reactions constituting the real problem are in your own thought. And it's right there in your own consciousness that the overcoming and enrichment take place.

KNOWING AND LIKING YOURSELF AND OTHERS

Is it possible to experience love, understanding, or friendship without expressing it? Can another's love truly reach you unless the love within you responds to it? If you are only thinking in terms of yourself, or in terms of someone to care for you, protect you, help you, and love you, it is like looking through the wrong end of a telescope. The love, friendship, or understanding that you seek seems out of reach. The friendship that satisfies your deepest yearnings is not a taking but a giving. It is not just an incoming affection but also your affectionate outreach. Instead of asking, "Why doesn't someone love and understand me?" you need to ask, "How can I express more love and understanding?" This may sound a bit sentimental for a text, but the love that we are speaking of is love in the universal sense, not physical love.

Deep within all of us is the psychological motivation to love and be loved, to communicate and be communicated with. Let's examine the statement, "Make a lover out of number one." What we are suggesting here is that you learn to know, like, accept, and love yourself first, and then you will naturally learn to know, like, accept, understand, and, yes, even love others. Since this desire is natural, your ability to reflect what you want in your experience is also natural. If a smile can be contagious, positive thinking and acting can also be contagious. If you endeavor to bring joy to a person, usually that person will reflect that process. If you stand in front of a mirror with a frown on your face, do not expect to get a smile from your reflection. People respond to your thoughts and actions in much the same way that your reflection responds to you in a mirror.

We allow others to be our mirrors; what we see is largely a reflection of their perception of us. Since we look to others for bits and pieces of our self-concept, what kind of mirrors are we holding for them to see themselves? Self-esteem is not self-procreating. We all work together on building each other's self-esteem.

Self-esteem is based on the self-image we desire. When we act, we expose a view of ourselves, whether intentionally or unintentionally. As a result, others respond to this behavior favorably or unfavorably. We tend to develop the behavior that receives positive responses and to use these responses as a measurement of self-esteem. This process is quite normal, when we consider that a child learns to like things about himself. "His self-esteem will reflect the amount of himself that he likes or accepts; to increase self-esteem he will tend to repress those parts of himself which he does not like."[1]

Often, if you enhance your self-esteem, that is all you need to do to be capable of viewing others differently. Since you rely on others to help you build your self-image, you need to remember that others depend on you to build theirs. If you can make a lover out of number one, you will probably be able to express more loving concern for others. You may wish to use the

[1] Kim Giffin and Bobby R. Patton, *Fundamentals of Interpersonal Communication* (New York: Harper & Row, 1971), p. 31.

Charles Gatewood.

Our   lives   are   shaped   by   those   who   love   us—

Stock, Boston

106   Beyond the World of Intra

by those who refuse to love us. —John Powell

following four skills to check your self-concept competencies; they are good tools to initiate, develop, and maintain effective interpersonal communication. Ask yourself these questions:

1. "Do I know and trust myself?" If you do, you can learn to know and trust others.
2. "Am I honest and explicit in understanding myself?" If so, you can be honest and explicit in understanding others.
3. "Am I able to influence my thinking and help myself?" If you answered yes, you can begin to influence and help others.
4. "Have I learned to resolve conflicts and cope with my world?" Is your answer yes? Then you can help resolve problems and conflicts constructively in your relationships with others.[2]

Each of these questions and its counterpart is a springboard from intrapersonal communication to interpersonal communication.

If you have learned anything from this text, you should be willing to be honest with others, willing to share, and able to care because you have examined your self-concept. You should have become aware of your perceptual structure, language usage, and consistency theories, and you should know how important having a positive self-concept is to successful communication.

Claim your true sense of individuality; mentally contradict useless declarations about yourself; reverse negative statements that others make about you. Accept the challenge to think and to rationalize problems clearly. Share your knowledge of self-concept with others; expect good results as you become more willing to share with and help others.

Because you are a unique individual, you express qualities in your own original way. Remember that others are also expressing themselves uniquely. You will see in others the good qualities you exhibit in your life. It is a natural reflecting process.

> I sit and I watch and I listen as
>   life drifts slowly by.
> And I wonder out loud just to
>   myself, "Who the heck am I?"
> Can I affect my future if I try?
> Everything I do seems to go awry.
> Is there nothin' more to life
>   than gettin' high?
>
> Who am I? Who are we?
> Am I you or are you me?
> Or are we both part of each other?
> And if we're not why would
>   any man call us brother?

[2] David W. Johnson, *Reaching Out* (Englewood Cliffs, N.J.: Prentice-Hall, 1973), p. 3.

I've always wanted to be somethin' else
A poet or singer or a movie star.
What is it about us that makes us
   what we are?
Why can't I ride a big white horse
   or sit in a racin' car?
Why are we what we are?

Who am I? Who are we?
Am I you or are you me?
Or are we both part of each other?
And if we're not why would
   any man call us brother?

—Bernie Schuneman
Speech 110 Student
(intrapersonal communication assignment)

SUMMARY   You should now be able to externalize your thoughts through interpersonal communication. In addition, intrapersonal communication is an ongoing process—it is never completed. Your self-concept should be constantly changing, and your concept of others should change in proportion to your acceptance of them. You should now be developing a willingness to share your thoughts of self-concept. You should also be willing to listen to others as they disclose themselves. Remember that, as others are mirrors of what you are, you hold a mirror for others to view themselves; you acquire self-esteem from interactions with others. You need to maintain your self-concept daily, and you need to develop trust intrapersonally and interpersonally. Accuracy in language usage should be a goal of interpersonal communication. Finally, you must establish your own individuality and recognize it in others. Remember above all that you are unique!

SUPPLEMENTARY READING

In this article from his text *Reaching Out*, David Johnson explains the need for self-acceptance as a natural corollary of interpersonal communication. To establish mature relationships, you must accept yourself before you can accept others.

ACCEPTANCE OF SELF AND OTHERS

David Johnson

In this article we focus upon accepting yourself and communicating acceptance to other people. The objectives of this article are to increase your self-acceptance and to increase your skills in expressing acceptance to others.

The Four Positions in Acceptance of Self and Others

Harris (1967) states that there are four possible positions held with respect to yourself and others. They are:

1. *I'm Not O.K., You're O.K.* In this position the person feels at the mercy of other people. He feels a great need for support, acceptance, and recognition. The person in this position hopes that others who are O.K. will give him support and acceptance, and he worries about what he has to do to get others to give him the support and acceptance he needs. He communicates to others that he is self-rejecting and needs their acceptance and support.

2. *I'm Not O.K., You're Not O.K.* In this position there is no source of support and acceptance, not from oneself or from others. Individuals in this position give up all hope of being happy and may withdraw from all relationships. Even if others try to give support and acceptance, the person in this position rejects it because they "are not O.K." He communicates to others both self-rejection and rejection of them.

3. *I'm O.K., You're Not O.K.* The person in this position rejects all support and acceptance from others, but provides it for himself. He feels that he will be all right if others leave him alone. He is ultra-independent and doesn't want to get involved with others. He also rejects the support and acceptance of others because they "are not O.K." He communicates to others that he is fine, but they are not.

4. *I'm O.K. You're O.K.* In this position the person decides that he is worthwhile and valuable and that other people are also worthwhile and valuable. He accepts himself and responds to acceptance from others. He can give acceptance and receive acceptance. He is free to get involved in meaningful relationships. He communicates to others that he appreciates his own strengths and appreciates their strengths. This is the position that everyone should strive to be in. This is the position which facilitates the development of close, meaningful relationships with others.

Every time you relate to another person you are communicating one of the above positions. Most people relate to everyone from the same position; that is, how they feel about themselves and others does not change greatly from relationship to relationship, and it governs everything they do. It is important for you to make the conscious decision that you are going to relate to others from the fourth position and strive to do that. Only when you accept yourself and accept other people can you build and maintain mature meaningful relationships.

Self-Acceptance

Self-acceptance is a high regard for yourself, or, conversely, a lack of cynicism about yourself. Generally, a high level of self-acceptance is reflected in a high level of quality of personal adjustment (see Hamachek, 1971). A person's mental health depends deeply on the quality of his feelings about himself. Just as an individual must maintain a healthy view of the world around him, so must he learn to perceive himself in positive ways. Psychologically healthy individuals see themselves as liked, wanted, acceptable to others, capable, and worthy. Highly self-critical individuals are more anxious, more insecure, and possibly more cynical and depressed than self-accepting individuals. The self-accepting person views the world as a more congenial place than the self-rejecting person and is less defensive towards others and about himself because of it. Carl Rogers (1951) considers self-acceptance to be crucial for psychological health and growth. It is not the individuals who feel that they are liked, wanted, acceptable to others, capable, and worthy who are found in prisons and mental hospitals; it is those who feel deeply inadequate, unliked, unwanted, unacceptable, and unable.

In order for you to grow and develop psychologically, therefore, you must be self-accepting. To help others grow and develop psychologically, you must help others become more self-accepting. To develop your potential for happiness and good relationships you must achieve and maintain a high level of self-acceptance. A self-rejecting person is usually unhappy and unable to form and maintain good relationships.

There is considerable evidence that self-acceptance and the acceptance of others are related (see Hamachek, 1971). Individuals who are self-accepting are usually more accepting of others. This means that if you think well of yourself you are likely to think well of others, and that if you disapprove of yourself you are likely to disapprove of others. In addition, things you try to hide from yourself about yourself you often are very critical of in others. A person who suppresses hostility may be highly critical of people who express hostility. A person who suppresses sexual feelings may be highly critical of individuals who are more open with their sexual feelings. If you recognize and accept your feelings, you are usually more accepting of such emotional expressions in others. The self-accepting person views the world as a more congenial place than the self-rejecting person and is less defensive towards others and about himself because of it. We will, then, be focusing upon how we may increase our self-acceptance and, therefore, become more accepting of others.

Your self-acceptance is built by knowing that others are accepting of you. The acceptance of you by others plays a critical role in increasing your self-acceptance, especially the acceptance of you by those you care about and respect. One of the ways in which you may become more self-accepting is to feel that other people whom you like and respect accept you. We will be focusing upon how to express acceptance towards others in order to help them increase their self-acceptance.

Your self-acceptance can set up self-fulfilling prophecies where your expectations concerning how other people are going to view you are actually confirmed as a result of your behavior. For example, a self-rejecting person expects to be rejected by others and will tend to reject others; as a result of his rejection, the people with whom he is interacting will reciprocate by rejecting him; the person's original expectations are then confirmed. A self-accepting person, on the other hand, will expect to be accepted by others and will tend to accept other people; they, in turn, will tend to reciprocate by being accepting of him; his original expectations are then confirmed. It is through such self-fulfilling prophecies that one may build good relationships or may experience real difficulty in making a friend.

To increase your self-acceptance, you must self-disclose in order to let other people know you and to experience acceptance by others. People are not accepting of individuals they do not know—most often they are neutral or indifferent. The relationship among self-acceptance, self-disclosure, and being accepted by other people is important. If you do not self-disclose, you cannot be accepted by others and your self-acceptance will not be increased. Paradoxically, not only is your self-acceptance increased by self-disclosing (and subsequently being accepted by others) but how easy it is for you to self-disclose is related to your level of self-acceptance. The greater your self-acceptance, the easier it will be for you to self-disclose. Self-confidence about your worth reduces the risks involved in self-disclosing. Self-acceptance is the key to reducing anxiety and fears about vulnerability resulting from self-disclosure. If you are afraid to let others know you, or anxious about the reactions others may have to your self-disclosure, you will not be open and disclosing, and, therefore, you will not be able to facilitate the development of good relationships with other people. If you are self-rejecting, you will find self-disclosure very risky.

The deepest conviction a self-rejecting person has is that once he is known he will be rejected and unloved. Before a self-rejecting person can have this conviction dissolved and experience more acceptance from himself and other persons, he must take the risk of disclosing himself. It is important for your self-acceptance that you are honest, genuine, and authentic in your self-disclosing. If you hide information about yourself or selectively try to create an impression on other people, the acceptance they give you may actually decrease your self-acceptance; you will know that it is your "mask" other people like and accept, not your "real" self. Being accepted for a "lie" leads only to self-rejection. It is only as you discover that you are loved for what you are, not for what you pretend to be or for the masks you hide behind, that you can begin to feel you are actually a person worthy of respect and love.

ADDITIONAL READING

Cole, Jim. *The Helpers*. Greeley, Colo.: Jim Cole, 1973.
A picture book on the individual's view of helpfulness. It encourages the understanding that people do need to be either helpless or helpful in order to grow with others.

―――. *The Controllers*. Fort Collins, Colo.: Shields Publishing Co., 1971.
A picture book dealing with our understanding of our responsibility in interpersonal relationships. It attempts to teach us to live without controllers and to understand that freedom comes with responsibility.

Harris, Sydney. *The Authentic Person*. Niles, Ill.: Argus Communications, 1972.
A unique graphic treatment of the individual's source of authenticity. It examines the difficulty of being a genuine person in a technological society and suggests that people must live creatively with polarities or remain where they are. It makes excellent reading for a new perspective on self-concept.

―――. *Winners and Losers*. Niles, Ill.: Argus Communications, 1968.
A book filled with succinct comments on self-image, values, motivation, and human relationships. The way a person views winning and losing influences basic attitudes about the self and others.

Gergen, Kenneth J. *The Concept of Self*. New York: Holt, Rinehart & Winston, 1971.
The search for the inner self. This book handles aspects of conscious worth, ego, and esteem, and it attempts to provide means for better self-understanding, grounded in empirical evidence.

Hamachek, Don E. *Encounters with The Self*. New York: Holt, Rinehart & Winston, 1971.
A collection of readings that focus specifically on the self as it is influenced by growth, teaching, learning, and perception. Selections also reflect the theoretical and philosophical bases underlying an understanding of self as a psychological frame of reference. Some readings are empirical studies, some are just speculative discussions, and others are analyses of trends and issues.

Krupar, Karen R. *Communication Games*. New York: Free Press, 1973.
A way for students to understand and evaluate their interaction with others. The initial groups of games deal with intrapersonal communication, while the following games deal with interpersonal relationships. The book provides stimulating exercises.

Prather, Hugh. *Notes to Myself*. Lafayette, Calif.: Real People Press, 1970.
An introspective view of one man's diary, and of how he maintains his self-concept from day to day. This interesting commentary encourages reconsideration of our own views of self-esteem and of our perspective on the surrounding world.

Stricker, George, and Michael Merbaum, eds. *Growth of Personal Awareness: A Reader in Psychology*. New York: Holt, Rinehart & Winston, 1973.
Selected readings dealing with the understanding and development of individual internalization. The book contains sections on such topics as principles of self-awareness, social contact, and individual growth.

INTRAPERSONAL
JOURNAL

JOURNAL EXERCISE 1

Self-Concept Sentence Completion

Begin your first step in self-examination with the sentence completion blanks that follow these instructions. You may wish to complete this journal entry three times as indicated below. This material is included as a journal entry because you may not be ready to share these personal and private thoughts.

First, record your immediate responses to the incomplete sentences on Sentence Completion Blank 1. Put this exercise away for a few hours. Then, without reference to your first set of responses, think intensively about each statement and write down your response on Sentence Completion Blank 2. Two days from now, complete the sentences on Sentence Completion Blank 3 and compare your three sets of responses. You may find that you really want to complete this exercise only once. The reason that we ask you to consider doing it three times is that moods, environmental conditions, and interpersonal relations may be such that you will gain new perspectives about yourself in the time lapse.

**Self-Concept
Sentence
Completion
Blank #1**

1. To be honest, I see myself as

2. The best word that describes me is

3. I'm happiest when I'm

4. To me, success in life means

5. One thing I'd like to prove to myself is

6. The school's (church's, family's) influence on me has been

7. The one thing I should do more often is

8. The thing I'd like to change about myself is

9.   The biggest threat in my life is

10.   The most important trait in a marriage partner is

11.   I think other people see me as

12.   Most of my attitudes toward people have been developed through

13.   My favorite trait in another person is

14.   When I enter a new relationship with someone, I'm afraid of

**Self-Concept
Sentence
Completion
Blank #2**

1. To be honest, I see myself as

2. The best word that describes me is

3. I'm happiest when I'm

4. To me, success in life means

5. One thing I'd like to prove to myself is

6. The school's (church's, family's) influence on me has been

7. The one thing I should do more often is

8. The thing I'd like to change about myself is

9. The biggest threat in my life is

10. The most important trait in a marriage partner is

11. I think other people see me as

12. Most of my attitudes toward people have been developed through

13. My favorite trait in another person is

14. When I enter a new relationship with someone, I'm afraid of

**Self-Concept
Sentence
Completion
Blank #3**

1. To be honest, I see myself as

2. The best word that describes me is

3. I'm happiest when I'm

4. To me, success in life means

5. One thing I'd like to prove to myself is

6. The school's (church's, family's) influence on me has been

7. The one thing I should do more often is

8. The thing I'd like to change about myself is

9. The biggest threat in my life is

10. The most important trait in a marriage partner is

11. I think other people see me as

12. Most of my attitudes toward people have been developed through

13. My favorite trait in another person is

14. When I enter a new relationship with someone, I'm afraid of

**JOURNAL
EXERCISE 2**

**The Self
as an
Art Object**

It has been said that life is reflected in a painting. If there were a portrait of you, what do you think other people would see in you as a study of life? To see yourself in this manner, stand in front of a mirror. Now answer the following questions:

1. What do you see about yourself?

2. Are you a happy person?

3. Does your face reflect confidence and quiet, or do you have a furrowed brow from worry or stress?

4. What does the mirror say about your posture, your dress, and your attitude about yourself?

5. How did you feel studying yourself in a mirror like an art object?

6. Do you think that other people who see you daily study you in this way or see the same things about you?

JOURNAL EXERCISE 3

Perceptual Evaluation

We hope that you will evaluate yourself by asking yourself the following questions:

1. In your own words, what does the expression *perceptual structure* mean to you?

2. Do you feel that you know yourself better from reading Chapter 2 and doing the exercises? Why is this important?

3. Which areas of your perception need to be improved?

4. Have we challenged your thinking? Do you just think that you think, or do you really think?

JOURNAL EXERCISE 4

Dissonance-Reducing Tactics

To discover what dissonance-reducing tactics you use and how you use them, answer the following questions:

1. What do you do with dissonance-producing information?

2. Which rationalizing tactics do you use most often?

3. How well do they work for you?

For the next three days observe your efforts to avoid or rationalize dissonant information; record the situations you encounter in the space provided on page 130. Note characteristics of the situations, the tactics you used to reduce dissonance, and your success in maintaining balance.

Situations with dissonant information:

**JOURNAL
EXERCISE 5**

**Language
Ambiguity**

During the next twenty-four hours, record each language failure in which you are involved. Include any exchanges where you are unable to recreate your internally experienced meaning in words for others, or where you are unable to create another's reference contexts from the word symbols. Could the two of you have avoided these situations if you had expended more energy to re-create each other's internal experiences? Do you think "meanings" ever pass between people, or do your words just collide with words?

Language failures

**JOURNAL
EXERCISE 6**

**Interpersonal
Communication
Evaluation**

To evaluate your interpersonal communication skills, answer the following questions:

1. How aware are you of what someone is saying to you in conversation?

2. Do you listen to people, or do you just think about what you are going to say next?

3. Doesn't it concern you that people might not be listening to you when you speak?

MISCELLANEOUS JOURNAL ENTRIES